Alternatives to Hollywood

A Teacher's Guide

Sarah Perks,
Isabelle Vanderschelden
and Andrew Willis

Auteur

Sarah Perks (East Asian New Wave Cinema)
is Education Director at Cornerhouse, Manchester.

Isabelle Vanderschelden (French Cinema)
is Senior Lecturer in French Studies at Manchester Metropolitan University. She is currently writing a critical study of Jean-Pierre Jeunet's film *Le fabuleux destin d'Amélie Poulain*.

Andy Willis (Indian Cinema)
is Senior Lecturer in Media and Performance at the University of Salford.

Acknowledgements

The publisher would like to thank Sarah Bemand and Andy Jeyes of Tartan Films for permission to reproduce the cover image, from *2046*.

£16.99

First Published 2005
by Auteur

Auteur

The Old Surgery, 9 Pulford Road, Leighton Buzzard, Bedfordshire LU7 1AB. Tel: 01525 373896
© Auteur Publishing, 2005

Except where indicated, stills are taken from the Region 2 DVD edition of the film under discussion: *Les 400 Coups* (c) Tartan Video; *Amélie* (c) Momentum Pictures; *Suzhou River* (c) Artificial Eye; *Monsoon River* (c) FilmFour.

Auteur on the internet: http://www.auteur.co.uk
Designed and typeset by AMP Design, 5 Pioneer Court, Chivers Way, Histon, Cambridge CB4 9PT
Printed by The Direct Printing Company, Saxon Fields, Old Harborough Road,
Brixworth, Northants, NN6 9BX

Contents

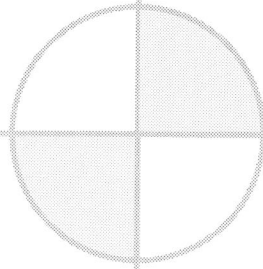

General Introduction

It is an informal requirement, at the very least, that today's teachers of Film and Media Studies are acquainted with non- Anglo-American cinema. This may be because of the demands of a particular syllabus, or a keen student who will expect her teacher to be able to engage with her enthusiasms. Perhaps you are teaching in an area where Indian films regularly occupy one or two screens at the local multiplex (such films now frequently appear in the UK Top Ten box office chart). For the Film and Media Studies teacher, it may be a steep learning curve, one which might be hampered at the very beginning through uncertainty as to exactly where to start.

This, then, was the inspiration for **Alternatives to Hollywood: A Teacher's Guide**. The **Guide** that follows does not claim to be exhaustive or all encompassing. It is an introduction and an overview of the cinemas of three nations/regions that are fairly commonly studied in post-14 formal education – France, India and, increasingly popular, East Asia. The aim is both to expand the understanding of the cinemas – with particular reference to the term 'New Wave' – while also discovering new films and film-makers to widen the scope of Film and Media Studies teaching and encourage students' curiosity about and knowledge of a wealth of foreign language film.

Most of the films discussed within are not 'art house' films – they are commercially successful, popular films, only classified as 'art house' in the UK because they are not in the English language. No teacher should feel afraid of using films from all over the world; after all, cinema is a universal visual language. Occasionally something gets lost in translation – colloquialisms of speech or local knowledge – but this is far outweighed by the intuitive recognition of the drama and emotions. It could be argued that an English audience could miss subtleties (perhaps because of accents) in a Scottish film - but few teachers would be afraid to use **Trainspotting** (1996) in the classroom. The aim for us all should be to offer a diverse range of extracts and case studies when teaching films, with a few at least offering students a taste of an alternative to Hollywood.

A note on style

This **Teacher's Guide** is the work of three writers who have all followed broadly the same approach, but whose styles differ in matters of detail. For example, while one might favour a textual analysis of a specific scene, another might prefer a more general consideration of a text's mise-en-scène. These stylistic differences have been retained so as to demonstrate the considerable scope for personal interpretation, and enjoyment, of texts; and also – and not unimportantly – to make the **Guide** more interesting for the reader.

But the basic approach remains the same. That is: a concise history of the cinema in question, followed by a more detailed analysis of particular periods, films or film-makers. Each chapter concludes with suggestions for teaching and a detailed bibliography and filmography to encourage further exploration.

Sarah Perks, Isabelle Vanderschelden and Andrew Willis

French Cinema

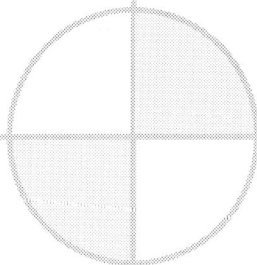

Introduction

The French like to think that cinema was officially born in France in 1895 with the first paying projection by the Lumière Brothers of the one minute film *La Sortie de l'usine Lumière/ Workers Coming Out of their Factory*. This highly symbolic landmark may partly explain why a century later, the French national cinema retains a strong identity and world presence, as the extensive centenary celebrations of cinema have confirmed throughout 1995, with numerous tributes, retrospectives and books.

At the dawn of the twenty-first century, the French cinema industry is the most prominent in Europe in terms of production and international presence. Other European cinemas tend to be confined to the margins of art cinema, even if Spanish cinema is currently going through a major revival. The European screens are in any case greatly influenced by the world domination of American cinema. In the last 20 years, approximately 170 feature films have been produced every year in France, with around 25 of these distributed abroad, following important changes in the film industry (e.g. concentration of the production network, increased role of television channels).

French cinema-going trends are also changing, transformed by the growing impact of young audiences and the decline of local cinemas, which are gradually being replaced by multiplex screens. In the last few years the expansion of the DVD market, the role played by pay channels like Canal+ and satellite film channels, and the introduction of monthly cinema passes which enable spectators to see as many films as they want for around £18 a month have also had significant consequences. Following a world trend, the number of French cinema spectators has declined dramatically from the 1950s to reach around 160 to 170 million a year today, with the market share of French films oscillating around 30% and 60% for the American production (CNC).

French cinema is exported to many countries (see CNC or Unifrance publications). In Europe, the situation is uneven, with a relatively high market share for French films in Germany, Belgium, Italy and Spain, etc. and decreasing interest in Great Britain. In the US, European films account for less than 2% of the box-office results, with at most half being French. In this respect, 2001 was an exceptional year, in terms of French box-office successes, both on the home market and abroad, with record numbers of foreign spectators for French productions (62M in 2001). The success of *Le fabuleux Destin d'Amélie Poulain/Amélie* (2001) was the most spectacular, but at least five other French films had a good reception at home (see Table 1, CNC).

French films with more than 3M domestic spectators in 2000-2001

Title	Audience (in millions)
Taxi 2	10.24
Amélie	8.85
La Vérité si je mens 2	7.46
Le Pacte des loups	5.58
Le Placard	5.29
Le Goût des Autres	3.80
Les Rivières pourpres	3.22
Yamakasi	3.22
Tanguy	3.03

Source: CNC – Bilan 2002

For these reasons, French cinema is sometimes seen as an alternative to the world domination of Hollywood cinema, not so much in terms of creating global blockbusters, but rather as producing a cinema that is different from Hollywood productions. French films project an art cinema image, and provide a window on a different culture, attracting specific audiences abroad, via the film festivals and independent art cinema circuits.

However, some aspects of the current national cinema are worrying. In the context of free trade and globalisation, the French film industry is becoming more concentrated at the expense of its diversity and financial independence (see Vivendi-Universal). For a number of years, the notion of cultural exception–'l'exception culturelle'–as applied to the French film industry, has been the subject of lengthy debate, and of a diplomatic crisis between France and the US at the time of the GATT agreements in 1993.

This section is therefore designed to offer Film Studies teachers and students an introduction to a number of specific aspects of French cinema which can be introduced in AS and particularly A2 modules (FS5), as well as current issues in contemporary French cinema.

Our aim here is to provide supportive information and resources to teachers, and to point to further reading and materials with which they can supplement this introductory survey. Within the framework of the module they may want to concentrate on one specific area, such as a period, a genre or a more theoretical aspect. For these reasons a number of resources have been included at the end, as we realise that we cannot provide an exhaustive overview of French cinema in a publication of this type which is meant as a practical guide rather than an academic essay.

The conceptual framework used includes aspects of production and reception, genre, *auteur* theory and also reference to national identity. After a short historical overview with a special mention of the New Wave period and its impact on contemporary cinema, a number of genres associated with recent French cinema are introduced. This is complemented by two case studies, which could be used in the classroom in different ways to illustrate relevant key issues: **Les 400 Coups** (1959) and **Le fabuleux Destin d'Amélie Poulain**.

N.B. The films in this section are quoted with French and English titles, year, and if relevant star and number of spectators in cinema in million (M). Unless indicated the sources used are the CNC tables, Powrie 1997, 1999 or Powrie and Reader 2002.

A Brief Historical Overview

Placing French cinema in its historical context is but one approach to studying its specificity. However, it constitutes a meaningful step for understanding some of the issues which will be discussed here, such as auteur cinema, mise-en-scène or cultural exception. The overview provided below is not meant to be comprehensive but to offer pointers which may be used in the classroom. Bibliographical information is indicated in brackets for further information.

(See also Austin 1996; Powrie and Reader 2002; Lanzoni 2002)

The origins of French cinema: Two approaches Lumière vs Méliès

(See Austin 1996; Hayward and Vincendeau 2000; Powrie and Reader 2002; Lanzoni 2002; and Crisp 1993)

Although the silent films of Auguste and Louis Lumière (1864-1948) and Georges Méliès (1861-1938) have pioneered the development of the early French film industry, we do not have the space here to do them justice. Nevertheless, French cinema is so rooted in the heritage of their experiments that it should be mentioned, however briefly. If the students are to concentrate on recent French cinema, it suffices to mention that Lumière and Méliès are often conveniently presented as the two opposite poles of cinematography at the turn of the twentieth century: a realist documentary approach for Lumière as opposed to a more creative, imaginary one for Méliès.

The Lumières started work in their father's factory in Lyons, and the thriving family business certainly helped them to finance the technical side of their experiments. From the work of the Lumières, the realist pole of the camera's function was derived, based upon the mechanical reproduction of visual reality. In this context, cinema acquired a documentary value ('actualités') through the clear description and recording of the world, e.g. *Sortie d'Usine* (1895), *L'Arrivée du train en gare de la Ciotat/ Arrival of the Train at La Ciotat* (1895), *Le Déjeuner de bébé/Baby's Lunch* (1895). The Lumières' films were so successful that they became the producers and distributors, as well as the directors, of about 1,000 films by 1898. It is worth noting that the films were carefully composed, with special attention to camera position, and that some were also based on a narrative, e.g. a standard joke in *L'Arroseur arrosé/ The Sprinkler Sprinkled* (1895).

Méliès was originally a stage person working on shows that involved magic and illusionist techniques. From 1896, he started screening films regularly at his theatre, thus discovering the camera's potential for distorting time and space, and for using special effects. He started making films which emulated the work of the Lumières, but soon developed a more formalist pole of film-making, whereby the camera was used to manipulate reality, by using special effects, trick photography and editing. A film can thus tell an unrealistic story, allowing the spectator to escape to a different world (e.g. *Voyage dans la lune/ A Trip on the Moon* 1902). In Méliès's films, the camera did not move (it was meant to represent the spectator and the spectator did not move), and the film medium was mostly used to serve the illusionist genius of its creator. Méliès developed a specific style through experimenting with 'mise-en-scène' techniques. He made 500 films between 1896 and 1912, and if his career ended in disaster (pirating of his work, inability to evolve, and bankruptcy), he remains a pioneer whose work represented a direct inspiration for Hollywood, not just in terms of special effects but also more generally in its escapist tendencies.

Thanks to the success of the pioneering work carried out by the Lumières and Méliès, the early French film industry was ahead of its time. This led to the development of two important French studios: Pathé and Gaumont, which dominated the film production market until the First World War, and still exist in different forms today.

The films of the 1920s were marked by an experimental trend, influenced by the artistic movements of the time (Impressionism, Dadaism and Surrealism), with directors often referred to as the French avant-garde. They included Abel Gance who favoured the visual in his films (e.g. *Napoléon* 1927), Louis Delluc who was credited with the development of film criticism and Jacques Feyder who initiated poetic realism.

Poetic realism in the 1930s

In 1927, the first talking film was produced in America (*The Jazz Singer*), and by the early 1930s silent cinema had become obsolete. This had important consequences for the film industry, especially in terms of the choice of stars and the use of screenplay and dialogue. A new era started for French cinema, often referred to as the classic era and a Golden Age, even though cinema became a nationally specific phenomenon, as it was more difficult to distribute talking films outside their country of origin. *Sous les toits de Paris/ Under the Roofs of Paris* (1930) is often judged to be the first mature talking film of this exciting period.

Following the 1929 world Depression, France experienced a period of increased political awareness, culminating in a populist movement, le Front populaire in 1935, with the first left wing government elected by the French people. It was followed by the deterioration of the European situation and the rise of fascism, which led to war in 1939. This context encouraged the development of poetic realism (le réalisme poétique), which characterises French cinema in the 1930s. A number of directors chose to film in a more documentary fashion, with a view to representing on screen ordinary characters in familiar surroundings. The intended effect of poetic realism was to project an ambivalent image, a romanticised vision of the world, as well as an atmosphere of fatalism reflecting the spirit of the time. These films rested upon a combination of 'peer' solidarity and love, pessimism and doom, and the unachievable aspiration of the characters to start a new life elsewhere. Death was usually the only possible ending. Popular stars of this period were Jean Gabin, Raimu, Pierre Fresnay, Michelle Morgan and Arletty.

Within poetic realism, a number of genres became established, especially comedies (Jean Renoir's *La Règle du jeu/ Rules of the Game* 1939) and literary adaptations (e.g. Zola's novels and Marcel Pagnol's plays). We have no space here to analyse the careers of Jean Renoir, Marcel Carné or Julien Duvivier as directors, Jacques Prévert or André Jeanson as scriptwriters, or Alexandre Trauner for sets but analyses of their work are available in English. Classic films such as *Pépé le Moko* (1937), *Le Quai des brumes/ Port of Shadows* (1938), *La Bête humaine/The Human Beast* (1938), or *Le Jour se lève/ Daybreak* (1939), which all represent the pre-war period and film style, have been the subject of many studies. It is important to appreciate how influential these films have been in the evolution of French cinema before the Second World War, in terms of stardom, technical and aesthetic development, auteurship, cultural heritage and national identity. They drew on a number of aspects of French culture, such as a popular form of musical theatre (théâtre de boulevard), the literary heritage, regional identity (Pagnol's Provence, Renoir and Carné's Paris) and class (Jean Gabin as the embodiment of the working class character). They also influenced the emergence of new genres, such as film noir after the war, and have inspired the evolution of French cinema to this day.

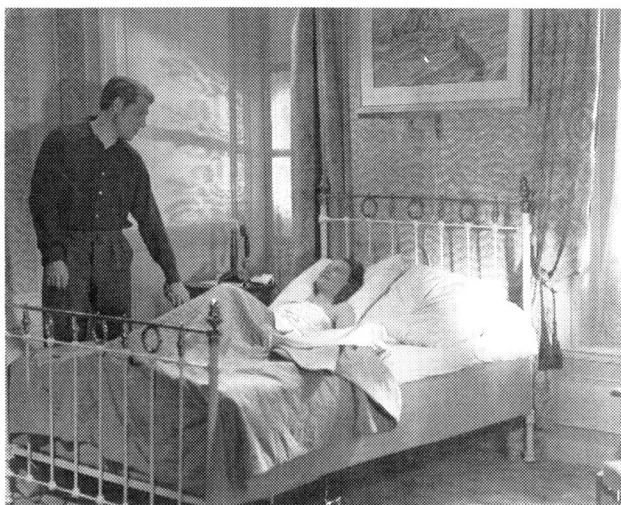

© BFI Stills

Jean Gabin and Michele Morgan in **Port of Shadows**

Post-war French cinema : Quality tradition and 'Cinéma de papa'

The Second World War seriously affected French cinema, although important films were made in the 1939-45 period. The Germans controlled French production, and many film-makers and actors emigrated to the United States (Clair, Renoir, Duvivier, Gabin, Morgan, Presle, etc.). However, American films were banned, which helped the French film industry to an extent. The Cinema of Occupation has left masterpieces like Carné's **Les Enfants du Paradis/ Children of Paradise** (1943-5, 4.7M).

(See Austin 1996; Powrie and Reader 2002; and Lanzoni 2002)

At the Libération, the cinema industry in France was seriously run down, and it took a while for film production to return to pre-war levels. Some French stars and directors had gone abroad and American films now flooded the French screens. But people needed entertainment more than ever, and by the early fifties, French production was thriving again, with films marked by distinctive characteristics that were then considered very quality oriented. Quality tradition ('la tradition de qualité') promoted the work of experienced directors including the following:

1. Julien Duvivier **Le petit Monde de Don Camillo** (1952, 12.8M).
2. René Clément **Jeux interdits** (1952, 4.9M).
3. Claude Autant-Lara **Le Diable au corps** (1947), **Le Rouge et le noir** (1954) and **La Traversée de Paris** (1956, 4.8M).
4. René Clair **Les Grandes Manoeuvres** (1955, 5.3M).

These films were the result of collaboration with renowned scriptwriters such as Jean Aurenche and Jacques Bost, and with established stars such as Jean Gabin, Gérard Philipe, Fernandel and Michèle Morgan. Their production costs were important as they developed specific conventions and canons, summarised below.

QUALITY TRADITION: FRENCH CINEMA CANONS IN THE 1950s

- Large budgets.
- Established stars.
- Literary/historical characters (archetypal heroes).
- Adaptations of classics (popular but little thematic originality).
- Traditional narratives (classical construction and plot).
- Domination of scripted dialogue (power of scriptwriter).

[Table 2: French cinema canons in the 1950s]

- Big production machinery (crew and equipment).
- Studio sets (artificial light and post synchronised sound).
- Heavy technical equipment (not very versatile).
- Commercial success and popular audiences (profitable, around 5-7M spectators).

The 'quality' productions of the post-war period benefited from strong audience support, as cinema was the main form of entertainment. By the mid-fifties, the productions were criticised for both their formalism and lack of innovation by the young critics of a newly founded 'Cahiers du cinéma' although this did not prevent quality directors from continuing to co-exist successfully with New Wave cinema in the 1960s.

(See Wiegand 1999; Monaco 1976; Wilson 1999; Lanzoni 2002; New Wave section in the Bibliography)

The French New Wave and its Impact on French Cinema

The French New Wave has become one of the most prominent 'movements' in the context of non-Hollywood cinema. New Wave directors have acquired international stature and their films are still readily available. The French New Wave has had a considerable influence on world cinema over the last 40 years, and has left an important legacy for subsequent generations of directors in France and beyond (e.g. Martin Scorsese, John Woo, Quentin Tarantino, Arthur Penn, Robert Altman). The New Wave has also been the subject of considerable critical and scholarly attention.

The young critics at 'Cahiers du cinéma'

(See Andrew 1990; Powrie and Reader 2002)

At the origin of the New Wave was a cinema journal 'Cahiers du cinéma' and the development of a critical notion 'la politique des auteurs', which both grew increasingly influential in the 1950s as a reaction to the mainstream 'quality tradition' on the one hand, and to enthusiastic cinephilic interest in a few distinctive directors working in Hollywood on the other (e.g. Hitchcock, Fritz Lang).

As early as 1948, a young director, Alexandre Astruc, wrote an influential article in the cinema journal 'L'Écran Français' entitled 'La caméra stylo' (the camera-pen), which associated the work of the film director to that of the writer. The young critics of 'Cahiers' later adopted this as a manifesto: the camera used as a pen creates its own unique language, and the images (and the dialogue) add nuance and develop the narrative.

In 1951, Jacques Doniol-Valcroze and André Bazin founded 'Cahiers du cinéma', which focused on film reviews and theoretical discussions, and was to play a major part in the evolution of critical analysis in the 1950s and the emergence of the New Wave (roughly 1958-68 – the end date of this New Wave is still debated). André Bazin, whose influence as a critic had been increasingly recognised since the forties, was also the one who introduced to 'Cahiers' a number of enthusiastic young intellectuals who wrote passionately about cinema: Eric Rohmer, Jean-Luc Godard, Alain Resnais, Claude Chabrol and François Truffaut. The latter was noticed as early as 1954 for a particularly virulent attack on contemporary mainstream French quality, which he renamed 'cinéma de papa' in an essay entitled 'A Certain Tendency of French Cinema' which criticised the uniform and unimaginative form of the dominant French productions of the time.

In the meantime, the intensive critical writings of the 'Cahiers' team focused on the work of specific directors/ auteurs, and on the 'mise-en-scène' strategies which identified their films. 'Mise-en-scène' (or stage direction) in this context refers to the shooting, camera use, actor direction, sequencing, editing and all aspects of filming. 'Cahiers' praised certain 'American' directors who refused to play the game of the Hollywood studios or looked to subvert traditional film-making from within, such as John Ford, Howard Hawks, Alfred Hitchcock and Fritz Lang who by then had moved to the US. They also analysed popular genres which had never been deemed worthy of critical attention (e.g. Westerns and B-movies). 'Cahiers' also supported some European directors, particularly the Italian neo-realists (Truffaut even worked for Rossellini), and provided new analyses of French classics such as the films of Jean Renoir and Jean Vigo. These films and their directors were defended brilliantly and wholeheartedly (with excessive zeal at times, as they recognised later), and they were to influence greatly the first films that Truffaut, Godard, Chabrol, etc. made at the end of the decade.

THE EMERGENCE OF THE NEW WAVE IN FRANCE: SUMMARY OF KEY DATES

1948 Alexandre Astruc's article: 'La caméra stylo' (camera-pen) *Écran Français*.
1951 Creation of *Cahiers du cinéma*.
1954 Truffaut's article 'A Certain Tendency of the

[Table 3: The emergence of the New Wave in France: summary of key dates]

French Cinema'. *Cahiers du cinéma* 31.
La Pointe courte (Varda).
1956 *Et Dieu créa la femme* (Vadim).
1957 Bazin's article 'De la politique des auteurs'
Cahiers du cinéma 70.
1958 Shooting of *Le Beau Serge* and *Les Cousins*
(Chabrol).
Shooting of *Les 400 Coups* (Truffaut). Death of André
Bazin.
Start of Fifth Republic. André Malraux Minister for
Cultural Affairs.
1959 *Les Quatre Cents coups* (Truffaut) and
Hiroshima mon amour (Resnais) presented at the
Cannes Festival.
Shooting of *A Bout de souffle* (Godard).

New Wave directors

Even though it has become a landmark in world cinema, the French
New Wave was not originally conceived as a cinema movement nor
a school, but rather was the result of specific socio-cultural
circumstances. A number of important technical developments (for
example, new, lighter cameras; faster, more light-sensitive film;
synchronous sound equipment and the advent of television), took
place in the second half of the 1950s, which coincided with the
emergence of a new generation of critics, actors and directors. The
phrase 'New Wave' was coined by a journalist (Françoise Giroud,
'L'Express' 1957) in the context of the emergence of the Fifth
Republic in 1958, and then used to define film production from
1959-60, but the movement was never really accepted by its main
protagonists – actors, scriptwriters and directors – who insisted on
the diversity of their individual artistic pursuits.

An important corpus of literature around the New Wave
directors is available in English, making it redundant here to try and
summarise the role of each member of the group of friends and
network of relations which played a central part in the New Wave's
first film explosion in 1958 and 1959. Suffice to say that the group of
new young directors who were included under the umbrella phrase
of the New Wave brought in new ideas, the enthusiasm of youth and
a sense of freedom into French cinema. Their different projects and
priorities may account for the diversity in the evolution of their
careers. Godard, for example, was the intellectual of the group

interested in formal experiments, and later became politically involved; Truffaut's films combined humanism, emotion and sensitivity; Rohmer developed a unique style close to literature and philosophical discourse; Resnais experimented with form, montage, time and space; while Chabrol embarked on a prolific, if uneven career mixing film noir and social satire.

New Wave directors functioned as a group, and one of the reasons why they were often considered as a movement was that they worked together, exchanging ideas, screenplays, technicians and even actors. This collaboration certainly helps explain some common characteristics in the films that were, and still are, associated with the New Wave.

It may be useful for students to compare Table 4 below with Table 2 as a measure of the radical changes in the New Wave directors' approach to film-making in narrative, thematic, technical and aesthetic terms:

FRENCH NEW WAVE CINEMA: SOME CHARACTERISTICS
New ways of filming
Relatively small budgets.
Co-productions and self-production.
New generation of young actors/ actresses playing young characters.
Original screenplays and/ or adaptations (*auteur*).
Personal tone and themes (*auteur*).
Modern tone.
Technical innovations at the service of the New Wave.
Natural sets/ location shooting.
Natural light.
New lighter cameras.
Reduced technical crew.
New Wave style
Improvised scenes or dialogue.
Unconventional narratives (e.g. non-linear, sequence shot, flashback, ellipsis).
Innovative editing (not necessarily based on continuity).
Reference to other cinemas (quotation).

[Table 4: French New Wave cinema: Some characteristics]

(See Caughie
1983, 1993;
Andrew 1990;
Wilson 1999,
Chapter 1)

The concept of 'auteur'

'La politique des auteurs' places the emphasis on the director, over
the star or the producer, which is a departure from the Hollywood
mainstream production tradition. Auteur theory developed in the 1950s
and became a central issue in the identity of New Wave directors – a
personal approach to film-making as critic André Bazin described it:

> The 'politique des auteurs' consists, in short, of choosing the
> personal factor in artistic creation as a standard reference, and
> then assuming that it continues and even progresses from one
> film to the next. (Bazin 1957)

As a result, **auteur criticism** has become a widely accepted – and
often unconsciously practised – film criticism method, which identifies
and examines a film by associating it with a director. Table 5 below
provides a schematic synthesis of possible *auteur*-based approaches,
summarising the ways in which an *auteur* approach can inform film analysis.

[Table 5: The
different
contexts of
auteur
cinema]

THE DIFFERENT CONTEXTS OF *AUTEUR* CINEMA
Auteurism: Artistic context
Director's personal vision of the world (not necessarily
autobiographical).
Active contribution of director to film production at
different levels.
Analogy between director and author.
Thematic and stylistic consistency in the director's work.
Relative independence of director.
Auteurism: Industry context
Art cinema image.
Experimental/ avant-garde cinema vs. commercial popular
cinema. Work of director/ artist vs. work of technician.
Relatively small budgets.
Auteur as a trademark of quality.
Director's name used as a marketing strategy.
Auteurism: Critical context
Associated with politique des *auteurs* of the 1950s
(Bazin, *Cahiers*).
Auteur cinema associated with New Wave cinema.
Evolution of auteur approach after the New Wave.

N.B. Most of the New Wave directors mentioned in this section
are still making films except Truffaut who died in 1984.

The legacy of the New Wave and *auteurism*

The legacy of the New Wave raises a number of issues: 40 years on, has an *auteurist* approach to French cinema become outdated, as some film theorists have argued since the 1980s? How has the concept of *auteur* cinema evolved?

(See Corrigan 1993 on the auteur approach)

The New Wave has transformed the image of French cinema, and has contributed to the promotion of an *auteur* cinema, in which the director is perceived as the author-creator of the text that the film represents. Nowadays, the qualifier of '*auteur*' attributed to a film-maker has gained a wider significance: *auteurs* have become first and foremost visible directors, directors who have achieved a coherent work ('oeuvre') in terms of filmography, creative input and recurring themes, stylistic characteristics, etc.

The two directors chosen as case studies may be introduced as examples of *auteurs* in separate and distinct ways: François Truffaut is a New Wave *auteur*, even if his work did evolve in the 1970s and 1980s; while Jean-Pierre Jeunet is an example of what can characterise an '*auteur*' director in the broader context of recent French cinema.

Auteur today remains a relevant approach to understanding French cinema in the following contexts:

THE CONCEPT OF *AUTEUR* CINEMA TODAY

[Table 6:The concept of auteur cinema today]

- **Auteur and an atypical production system in terms of:** funding (small budget, partly subsidised and specific production network); distributing (limited exposure and art cinema networks); directing (relative freedom of director).
- **Auteur and the coherence of the director's work:** image projected (e.g. a Chabrol or a Rohmer film); notion of film 'family' (e.g. Chabrol and Isabelle Huppert); emphasis on personal artistic project; posterity.
- **Auteur and style:** emphasis on *mise-en-scène* and originality; cinema as art.
- **Auteur and reception:** auteur film as an alternative to mainstream popular cinema; *auteur* cinema as an alternative to a genre approach.
- **Auteur and national cinema:** construction and consolidation of national identity; *auteur* film as an international showcase for French cinema.

Case Study: *Les 400 Coups/400 Blows* (Truffaut, 1959)

There are several reasons for choosing **Les 400 Coups** for the New Wave case study. It is, together with **A Bout de souffle**, the most representative film of the start of the New Wave in France, and one of the most important films of that period.

Les 400 Coups is the first feature film of acclaimed director François Truffaut, whose career illustrates the notion of *auteur* cinema discussed above. Not only does it set the scene for Truffaut's approach to film-making, but it introduces many of the recurring themes developed in his films, and it can therefore be seen as a matrix for his filmography (Gillain 1991).

Les 400 Coups is an accessible film, rediscovered with interest generation after generation. It is very popular with students, and lends itself well to a detailed thematic and stylistic analysis. The film has inspired numerous French and non-French directors. More than 40 years after its release, it is still viewed as a landmark in French cinema, which has retained its freshness and emotional force.

François Truffaut

© Joel Finler Archive

(See de Baecque and Toubiana 1999; and Insdorf 1994)

Truffaut's life was a major source of inspiration for his films, which justifies this biographical summary. He had a troubled childhood shared between an unloving mother, a step-father and a grandmother with whom he spent a great deal of time. He never met his birth father although he tried to find him as an adult, and the mystery surrounding his real identity was to pursue him all his life, being a central issue in some of his films.

Truffaut looks back on his childhood as the most disastrous period of his life, which partly inspired **Les 400 Coups**. He came back to live with his mother in Paris near Pigalle and Montmartre at the age of ten. As a young boy, he was often left on his own, and he shared his time between reading and going to the cinema. He even started a cine-club with his best friend René Lachenay at the age of 14. After a troubled time at school, and a period spent in a young delinquent centre, he joined the French army, which he soon deserted, resulting in a prison sentence.

During his unstable teenage years, Truffaut had developed an impressive cinematic culture. The established film critic André Bazin, whom he had met through a cine-club, took him under his wing, helped to secure his release from prison and encouraged his interest in film. In the 1950s, Truffaut lived mostly with the Bazins, and started writing a number of influential critical essays for 'Cahiers du cinéma', in which he directly attacked the celebrated directors of French cinema of the period and the tradition de qualité that they represented. Behind this critical stance was a new vision of cinema, which placed the director at the centre of the film creation process, and ultimately led to the emergence of the New Wave in 1959. Truffaut's writings of that period also included brilliant analytical essays, praising the films of directors like Jean Renoir, Howard Hawks, Orson Welles and Alfred Hitchcock who, he felt, were unjustly underestimated, as he viewed them as true *auteurs*. Truffaut's role was therefore crucial in the development of an *auteurist* approach to cinema known as '*la politique des auteurs*'. He became closely acquainted with a group of young critics, including Alain Resnais, Eric Rohmer, Jean-Luc Godard and Claude Chabrol, who played an active part in launching and developing his career as a film-maker.

From the mid-fifties onwards, Truffaut's life became closely linked to his films and the development of his career. As a well known, if controversial, film critic and leading New Wave director, Truffaut devoted his life to making over 20 films which reflected his three passions: his relationship with women, his fascination with children and most importantly, his passionate love of cinema.

In the mid-fifties, he started directing shorts films – **Les Mistons** in 1957 is considered the first real step of his cinematographic work – and he worked as an assistant to directors like Max Ophuls and Roberto Rossellini. The year 1957 was important from a personal viewpoint, as he married Madeleine Morgenstern, the daughter of an important film distributor, and founded his own production company 'Les Films du Carrosse'.

In 1959, he became a father, and completed his first feature film, **Les 400 Coups**, the first of the Antoine Doinel series. The film, which has now become a classic of French cinema, is heralded as one of the most representative examples of the New Wave production values. It was an instant popular and critical success, and it established Truffaut's international reputation, whilst securing financial independence for his next projects. Truffaut later continued to film Doinel's youth and adulthood in five other films, including **Baisers Volés/ Stolen Kisses** (1968), **Domicile conjugal/ Bed and Board** (1970), **L'Amour en fuite/ Love on the Run** (1979), all featuring Jean-Pierre Léaud who was to become the film-maker's alter ego. These films have a special place in Truffaut's filmography, as they create a mythical hero and illustrate the strong personal element inherent to *auteur* cinema, deriving from the New Wave.

From the early 1960s, Truffaut expresses himself through narrative fiction and his work alternates between original screenplays and adaptations, and also between personal films and more light-hearted ones. These films include: **Tirez sur le pianiste/ Shoot the Pianist** (1960), a parody of B-movies which was a commercial flop; **Jules et Jim** (1961), which defines the modern romantic triangle, through the bittersweet story of Jules, Jim and Catherine (Jeanne Moreau), the woman who dominates their lives and refuses to choose (whilst slightly scandalous, the film was a public success); **La Peau douce/ The Soft Skin** (1964) is a stern anatomy of adultery not unrelated to the breakdown of his own marriage; **La Mariée était en noir/ The Bride Wore Black** (1968) represents his most explicit homage to Hitchcock and film noir; **La Sirène du Mississippi/ Mississippi Mermaid** (1969, with Deneuve); and in **L'Enfant sauvage/ The Wild Child** (1969), Truffaut himself took the part of the doctor obsessed with understanding how to communicate with a boy who grew up away from society.

By the end of the 1960s, Truffaut's New Wave image is less clearcut and he is sometimes perceived as not having sustained his commitment to new forms of cinema. He seems to return to a more conventional style of filming. Although he played a part in the events of May 1968 with the Langlois affair, Truffaut kept his distance from the sociopolitical context of the time, and went through a difficult time for the next five years, experimenting with a variety of styles and genres.

La Nuit américaine/ Day for Night (1973) is an exuberant celebration of the joy of film-making. It depicts the crew as a sort of family, and illustrates Truffaut's approach to cinema in a near documentary fashion. It marked a return to popular success and received an Oscar.

L'Histoire d'Adèle H/ The Story of Adele H (1975, with Adjani) is a historical drama about Victor Hugo's daughter; *L'argent de poche/ Small Change* (1976) is a joyous depiction of childhood; *L'Homme qui aimait les femmes/The Man Who Loved Women* (1977) is a celebration of women and love; while *La Chambre verte/The Green Room* (1978) is a personal study on the subject of death. All these films demonstrate a conscious attempt at stylisation and a rejection of television production values.

In 1976, Truffaut accepted the invitation of Steven Spielberg to star in *Close Encounters of the Third Kind* (1977) as the scientist in search of communication with extra-terrestrials.

Le dernier Métro/ The Last Metro (1980, with Depardieu and Deneuve) and *La Femme d'à côté/ The Woman Next Door* (1981, with Depardieu and Ardant) feature love triangles (the former in the context of the theatre and the Second World War, the latter in a contemporary setting); *Vivement Dimanche/ Confidentially Yours* (1983) parodies American film noir and thrillers. While *The Last Metro* finally brought Truffaut unanimous acclaim with ten Césars and his best commercial success, it is probably *The Woman Next Door* which is the most accomplished film that Truffaut made from a stylistic viewpoint.

Always concerned with film as process and also as product, Truffaut retained his role as critic and commentator throughout his film-making career, being as proud of his books as he was of his films. Among his publications is a book-length interview with Hitchcock, 'Hitchcock-Truffaut' (1967); his critical essays were collected in 'Les Films de Ma Vie/ The Films of My Life' (1975), and his letters posthumously in 'François Truffaut: Correspondance' (1990).

All Truffaut's films are characterised by thematic continuity, but mostly by a desire to give the director total artistic freedom.

Truffaut died suddenly of a brain tumour in 1984, leaving a number of projects in progress.

The film

(See Gillain 1991; Gillain 2000; and Insdorf 1994)

Les 400 Coups is based on a screenplay written by Truffaut himself and Marcel Moussy. It was mostly shot on location in Paris over eight weeks in 1958 with a 37 million Francs budget, which was a roughly a third of the average cost of a 'quality' film of the 1950s. It was produced by Truffaut's new company, Films du carrosse, and with funding from his father-in-law.

Les 400 Coups was a great commercial and artistic success, even though Truffaut as a critic had upset the critical establishment of the 1950s and little leniency was expected for his first film. Following its French success, the film was released in many countries including the US and the selling of the rights alone covered the cost of the film. It was presented at Cannes in 1959 (Prix de la mise-en-scène) and was shown exclusively in Paris for 14 weeks. Viewed by 450,000 spectators in France, it was one of the most successful films of the period.

It is always difficult to assess why a film is successful, but Anne Gillain (1991: 5) points at three main factors: the theme of adolescence, the choice of actor and a key moment of the late 1950s. ***Les 400 Coups*** also reflects the dynamic force of new aesthetic values, as we will see below. More importantly the success of his first film gave Truffaut the professional recognition and financial independence that he needed to pursue a career in *auteur* cinema.

Synopsis

Antoine Doinel is a 12-year-old Parisian boy growing up in the 1950s in a tiny flat with his mother and step-father who neglect him. He is unhappy at home and he does not enjoy school, where he always seems to find himself in trouble. Playing truant with his best friend René, he accidentally sees his mother embracing a stranger in the street. The next day, needing an excuse for his absence, he tells the teacher that his mother is dead. His parents find out about the lie, and he decides to leave home, only to return the next day. For a while, his mother seems to change, taking him to the cinema, but it does not last. Antoine finds refuge at his friend René's house, but he needs money. He steals a typewriter from his step-father's office, and failing to find a buyer for it, tries to return it only to be caught by the security guard. Following a visit to the police station where he is charged for theft and vagrancy, his parents don't want anything to do with him and he is sent to a juvenile detention centre. After a revealing conversation with a psychologist, Antoine runs away from the centre and goes to the seaside.

Main themes and style

Themes

Les 400 Coups is set in the context of 1950s France and can be read as the representation of a period (end of the Fourth Republic, education system, housing, etc.). In this respect, it illustrates a desire for more realism and documentary input in film – 'pure document' in Truffaut's words, which is characteristic of New Wave cinema.

The film raises more universal preoccupations which can also be found in other Truffaut films. The central themes of *Les 400 Coups* include the joys and difficulties of childhood, the complex relationship with women/ mother, the crisis of masculinity and fatherhood, the quest for freedom, the rebellion against authority, and a passionate relationship with artistic creation and writing. Again, some of these themes correspond to the longing for freedom and self-expression often associated with the New Wave. They are mostly developed around the main character Antoine, a child confronted by the world of the adults (parents, teacher, police, psychologist, etc.). Antoine is depicted as a neglected child, but also as creative and full of initiative. Unfortunately, his actions always seem to lead to disaster (the pin-up photograph means detention, the exciting essay becomes plagiarism, the shrine to Balzac nearly ends in a fire, the truancy leads to the lie about his mother's death, the theft of the typewriter leads to the delinquent centre).

As the psychologist scene shows, most of Antoine's misadventures are related to his problematic relationship with his mother. He knows that he was not wanted, because she neglects and ignores him. She even humiliates and rejects him on several occasions. Yet, he longs so much for her attention that he 'symbolically' pronounces her dead.

Autobiographical elements

The film has often been studied from the view point of autobiographical similarities between the young Truffaut and Antoine which tend to be confirmed by Truffaut's biography (Gillain 2000). Truffaut admits that the characters and situations of *Les 400 Coups* are true, if not strictly autobiographical. However, it is important to note that the film is a work of fiction in which the action and characters are transposed, while events are stylised and selective. Truffaut's intimacy with his subject matter adds to the humanity and emotional impact of the narrative. The film is certainly influenced by personal experience and, as such, illustrates the notion of *auteur* cinema in which the director transposes a personal vision of the world.

Narrative

Truffaut is a sentimental director. His films focus on characterisation and human relationships. They often contain an element of melodrama, with an emphasis on the complexity of love relationships. In *Les 400 Coups* the narrative, which is deliberately fragmented and elliptical, focuses on Antoine, who is rarely off the screen and represents the subject of the film. *Les 400 Coups* does not dwell on action and events, but rather promotes the creation of a specific atmosphere around the notion of spiral and vicious circle. In this respect the theft of the typewriter is a key moment as it marks the branding of Antoine as a delinquent.

Anne Gillain summarises the distinctiveness of Truffaut's narratives in three key words: **economy, concentration** and **efficiency** (1991: 100). He avoids gratuitous effects and unnecessary shots. A close study of *Les 400 Coups* shows that every detail serves the guiding line of the narrative and reinforces its internal coherence.

Mise-en-scène

Visually speaking, the film rests upon an opposition between two different types of space: indoor and outdoor, which punctuate the rhythm of the film. The interior scenes at home, at school and in the delinquent centre evoke confinement and oppression. **Static** and **close-up shots** are used to highlight confrontation and lack of freedom. Conversely, the exterior scenes in the streets of Paris – that Antoine clearly loves – or at the sea – that he has never seen – emphasise open space, using **wide-angle, mobile** and **open shots**, generating an impression of freedom associated with Antoine's imagination and his longing for self-expression. In these scenes, Antoine is alive and free to assert his identity. Outside he can relax and escape reality (e.g. the scene of the rotor); indoors, he is like a prisoner, which generates tension.

The film is shot in Cinemascope, which is unusual and original in the context of an explicitly non-spectacular black and white film, as 'Scope, which appeared in Hollywood in 1953, is often associated with colour and big budgets. Truffaut has justified this format by the need for an opening of space on the screen, to create the spatial dichotomy that has just been discussed, to contrast the use of black and white film and the grim setting of the film, with a more aesthetic project in which the child's imagination transforms the reality through more stylised images (Gillain 1991: 106). This choice contrasts with the deliberately careless look of Godard's *A Bout de souffle*.

If *Les 400 Coups* has often been considered as representing the epitome of New Wave values and the result of a critical and artistic movement, other influences should also be mentioned. The film's intertextuality, with influences as diverse as Vigo's *Zéro de conduite/ Zero for Conduct* (1933) or Rossellini's *Germany Year Zero* (Rossellini 1947), reinforces Truffaut's reputation as an erudite passionate cinephile and informs on his personal vision of what cinema is.

Study of individual scenes

Key Scene 1: Antoine at home (DVD chapter 3)

Context: This is the second major scene of the film. It has an important presentation value, as the spectator discovers important information which clarifies the narrative in a very economical but powerful form. Antoine steals money from his mother, who ignores her son or treats him like a servant. She openly admits that she hates children, and the relationship between the two parents is based on conflict and aggression. There is no display of affection/ love in the household.

Main themes: These are exclusion, the mother-son relationship and the disintegrated family unit. Antoine feels excluded at home, because of the indifferent and even hostile attitude of his parents, who neglect and dehumanise him. The Doinels live in a small flat where Antoine has no place: he does not have his own room and sleeps on a camp bed set up every night in the hall, he is considered a burden and a source of trouble.

Style: The confined space of the flat shot with a static camera and limited lighting is associated with imprisonment, apprehension and restraint – just as are the other interior locations of the film (classroom, police station, etc.). These scenes contrast with the freedom expressed in the outdoor scenes in the Montmartre streets, which are shot with a mobile camera including panning, tracking and long shots. The visual lightness also creates a different atmosphere, which echoes Antoine's energy and freedom.

Space is used in the film to communicate information. It acts as a metaphor of Antoine's situation: he is inhibited and a victim of adult authority at home, at school, at the police station and in the centre. In these scenes, the fixed close-up shots of Antoine highlight his problematic relations with the adults of the film, which are all based on authority (except the psychologist). In contrast, Antoine is free to unwind and express his youthful energy in the streets of Paris with his friend René, and at the fair on his own.

This scene can therefore be used to illustrate how camera work creates meaning as well as plot or dialogue.

Key Scene 2: The conversation with the psychologist (DVD chapter 18)

Context: Towards the end of the film, Antoine is interviewed by a psychologist at the detention centre. His friend warns him that anything he says is likely to be misinterpreted on his file. Antoine sits facing the camera in medium close-up throughout. The set is neutral, there are no props. The psychologist is off screen and simply asks questions. The scene was unscripted and mostly improvised to encourage spontaneous responses, with Léaud's natural hesitations and his own words.

This scene can be analysed from different perspectives depending on which aspect of the course it illustrates:

- It is a key scene in the **narrative structure**, as it represents the only opportunity that Antoine is given to express himself freely. It is also the scene in which an attempt is made at explaining Antoine's crisis of identity, and his difficult passage from childhood to adolescence. It contrasts with other scenes in the film where Antoine is passive and dominated by the presence of others (e.g. the last visit of his mother at the centre).
- The scene can lend itself to a **thematic study** of the film's issues, such as Antoine's relationship with adults, particularly with his mother.
- The scene can also be studied from the perspective of *mise-en-scène*. The interview form was commented upon by many critics as representative of **New Wave style**, excluding traditional film representation (shot/ reverse shot), and almost approaching a pure documentary form. It is also an exercise in editing, experimenting with **fade-ins** for a fluid temporal continuity.
- The scene illustrates the relationship between dialogue and documentary style. Antoine is at ease, and for the first time, free to express himself verbally. He uses colloquial vocabulary and spontaneous orality markers. He shows how articulate, inventive and full of life he naturally is.

Key Scene 3: The final scene (DVD chapter 20)

Context: Having escaped from the centre Antoine is seen running in a long sequence shot until he arrives at the seaside and realises a dream – seeing the sea.

Themes: This final sequence is complementary to key scene 1, and lends itself well to a comparative study. It can be analysed from the viewpoint of the thematic lines developed in the film, i.e. freedom and confinement. Antoine clearly expresses his energy for life running towards the sea, which can be read as a metaphor of freedom and the end of his childhood. However, Antoine may be free, but he is also alone and cannot go any further.

The **stylistic** innovation of this last scene is well worth commenting upon. The scene is one long, regular **sequence shot**. Antoine runs for over 90 seconds, and the camera follows him in a fluid **tracking shot**, which emphasises physical effort. Time seems to disappear, and the spectator is left with only the present moment. The space gradually opens up for Antoine who finally faces the ocean. He is stopped in his tracks by the water and draws breath. Then he faces the camera, which gradually zooms in. His eyes are bright, his expression is ambiguous, and the film ends on an innovative **freeze-frame close-up** of Antoine's face looking at the camera. The musical score written by Jean Constantin is particularly emotional at this stage.

The last scene illustrates the concept of **closure** in cinema. In fact, here it conveys a *lack* of closure, an open ending, which is characteristic of New Wave *auteur* values. The spectator's gaze cannot stray from the **freeze-frame** image of Antoine on the screen, which can be interpreted in different ways. What will happen to Antoine is impossible to say. But there remains the powerful image of a child suddenly maturing. Antoine has left his childhood behind him, and we are left with an impression of new beginning, of rebirth at the place where the sand and the sea meet. One thing is clear: nothing more will happen, the fiction is over and the spectator has to let go (for further discussion of the ending see Raskin).

Contemporary French Cinema Trends

Contemporary French films are characterised by specific (but also hybrid) genres, which have gradually become associated with French cinema's national identity. In the 1980s and 1990s particularly, France's cinema has explored, redefined and promoted genres as different as comedy, social-realist drama, 'intimist' film, historical epic, banlieue film and thriller. The last two decades have also been marked by the increasing influence of female directors, and of a new generation of young film-makers ('young French cinema') who have marked a return to social realism. Mathieu Kassovitz's *La Haine/ Hate* (1995), Erick Zonca's *La Vie rêvée des anges/ Dream Life of Angels* (1998) are only two influential examples of this new trend.

Given the space constraint, we have chosen to present four significant genres, representative of the evolution of French cinema in the last 20 years:

- The emergence of heritage film in the 1980s and 1990s.
- Two traditional popular genres: policier film and comedy.
- And a French specific genre for the 1980s: 'film du look'.

A genre approach can facilitate comparisons between Hollywood and French cinema. However, specific conventions can also be the starting point for a detailed study of a given French film from a genre perspective, and can inform on French and foreign audiences expectations. Genre can help students to identify and analyse non-Hollywood cinema, and will complement other perspectives, such as European art cinema or auteur cinema.

Heritage film

Definition

Heritage films are mostly quality period dramas drawing upon French national and cultural identity as represented in cinema. They are characterised by lavish spectacular (super) productions, classical form and narrative, and often rely on familiar stars to attract a wide audience. In France, they are directly associated with the notion of patrimony ('films du patrimoine'), and explicitly draw upon the cultural heritage of the nation, namely the literary heritage, history, the arts, the use of language, and even the regional culture. They also

(See Austin 1996, Chapter 7; Powrie 1997, Chapter 2; and Wilson 1999, Chapter 6)

25

A vehicle for French national identity

Heritage films are usually endowed with a mission of dissemination and promotion of the French cultural identity at home and abroad. This is achieved in the following ways:

1. Authenticity of their subject matter which legitimised their sources (literature, history, art, etc.).

2. Emphasis on the geographical location of the films, for example, Paris, Provence and Britanny.

3. High-profile stars like Gérard Depardieu, Catherine Deneuve, Isabelle Adjani, Daniel Auteuil and Juliette Binoche.

tend to promote nostalgia and may be associated with the intimist period melodrama, which focuses upon psychological character study (e.g. *Un Coeur en hiver* 1992).

Even though the national cultural heritage was already present in the cinema of the 1930s (poetic realism) and of the 1950s (quality tradition), the heritage film genre in France is mainly associated with the 1980s/1990s for a number of reasons, some artistic and some more commercial. The political and cultural context of the 1980s played a significant part in the development of heritage film in France. Socialist Cultural Affairs Minister Jack Lang's cultural policy (1983-6) encouraged the financing and promotion of French productions, reinforcing a subsidy-based system, unique to France, which, since 1959, had helped to finance films partly by a tax received on every cinema ticket sold which is allocated to French films ('avance sur recette'). Lang's policy (and funding) helped to revive the French film production and favoured mainstream quality films, which drew on the French national heritage ('high culture for the masses'). His policy of democratisation of cultural cinema (1986), also aimed at countering Hollywood's growing imperialism on French screens, was a turning point, although American films overtook French films in terms of domestic market share from 1986.

Heritage films were popular successes in France, but they were also destined for an international career, mainly via the film festival and art cinema circuits. These films also increasingly led to co-production enterprises between different European film companies, and the development of the heritage trend may have contributed to a European film identity and a revival of the notion of European cinema in the last 20 years.

Heritage films consolidate the international scope of French cinema, as they tend to fulfil the foreign spectator's expectations in terms of stereotypes and the representation of national identity. They have played an important part in the construction of French cinema's identity in the 1980s and 1990s, even if they have not always had the expected reception.

Examples of French heritage films in the 1980s and 1990s

- Adaptations of literary classics: *Germinal* (Berri 1993, 6.1M); *Le Colonel Chabert* (Angelo 1994); *Madame Bovary* (Chabrol 1991); *Cyrano de Bergerac* (Rappeneau 1990, 4.7M); Pagnol's *Jean de Florette* (Berri 1986, 7.2M); *Manon des sources* (Berri 1986,

6.6M); *La gloire de mon père* (Robert 1990, 6.2M) and *Le Château de ma mère* (Robert 1990, 4.2M).

* Modern fiction: *Sous le soleil de Satan* (Pialat 1986) and *L'Amant/ The Lover* (Annaud 1992, 3.1M).
* Historical films: *Indochine* (Wargnier 1991, 3.2M); *Tous les matins du monde* (Corneau 1992, 2.1M); *La Reine Margot* (Chéreau 1994); *Le Hussard sur le toit/ Horseman on the Roof* (Rappeneau 1995); *Ridicule* (Leconte 1996); *Les Destinées sentimentales* (Assayas 2000) and *Saint Cyr* (Mazuy 1999).
* War films: *Lacombe Lucien* (Malle 1974); *Au Revoir les enfants* (Malle 1987, 3.5M); *Lucie Aubrac* (Berri 1996) and *Monsieur Batignole* (Jugnot 2002); *Un long dimanche de fiançailles/ A Very Long Engagement* (Jeunet 2004)
* Art biography/bioepic: *Van Gogh* (Pialat 1991); *Sade* (Jacquot 2000) and *Camille Claudel* (Nuytten 1988, 2.7M).
* Intimist period films: *Un Dimanche à la campagne/ Sunday in the Country* (Tavernier 1980) ; *Un Coeur en hiver* (Sautet 1992); *Le parfum d'Yvonne/ Yvonne's Perfume* (Leconte 1994); *La Veuve de Saint Pierre/ The Widow of Saint Pierre* (Leconte 1999); *Les Choristes/ The Choir* (Barratier 2004).

'Film policier' or 'polar'

Definition

'**Film policier**' or '**polar**' defines a broad genre in French national cinema, including any film constructed around criminal activity, murder and thriller, and does not always involve the police. Film policier may also be associated with comedy, action and adventure film, thriller or psychological drama.

(See Austin 1996, Chapter 5; Powrie 1997, Chapter 9)

The 'policier' genre has represented a major contribution to the French cinematic production since the 1920s, yet it has largely consisted of a culturally specific popular tradition. As a result, policier films have received limited international attention, until the revival of B-movies associated with the New Wave, and the international successes of 'film du look' in the 1980s and 1990s. The films mentioned below are representative of different periods. They are examples of classics in France, domestic box-office successes or films which have been widely distributed abroad.

N.B. *The policier
genre in the
1990s has also
drawn its
inspiration from
Hollywood
cinema:* **Leon**
(1994); **Taxi**
(1998, 6.4M);
Taxi 2 *(2000,
10.2M); and*
**Les Rivières
pourpres/
Crimson Rivers**
(2000).

Short survey of French policier film

1950s:
Classic popular films - adaptations of American and
French crime fiction (Série noire). Key stars: Jean Gabin
and Lino Ventura, e.g. **Touchez pas au grisbi** (1954).
Emphasis is placed on masculinity.

1960s-1970s: Three main trends can be highlighted:
• Influence of New Wave (B-movies), e.g. **A bout de
  souffle/ Breathless** ; and **Tirez sur le pianiste/ Shoot
  the Pianist**.
• Popular 'polar' linked to comedy and adventure with an
  emphasis on screenplays (Michel Audiard) and familiar
  stars like Jean-Paul Belmondo and Alain Delon, e.g. **Le
  Samourai** (1967); and **Borsalino** (1970, 4.7M).
• Post-1968 influence: political thrillers/policier films, e.g.
  Z (1969, 3.9M).

1980s-1990s:
• Atmospheric *auteur* films: **Vivement Dimanche/ Finally
  Sunday** (1984); **Poulet au vinaigre** (1985); and
  Monsieur Hire (1988).
• Beur cinema and banlieue film: **La Haine**.
• Social realism: **Police** (1985); and **L.627** (1992).
• More stylised 'films du look': **Diva** (1981); and **Subway**
  (1985).
• Popular comedy/ action thrillers: **L'As des as** (1982,
  5.4M); **Les Ripoux** (1984, 5.8M)

French comedy tradition

Like policier film, comedy has always been central to the French
popular film production, and it has over the years contributed to a
variety of classics and cult films, which are part and parcel of the
French popular heritage. Until the 1970s, comedy relied on star
actors, such as Louis De Funès, Bourvil and Fernandel, their
objective being to entertain a family audience. However, towards the
end of the 1970s, a new generation of actors and writers initiated a
move toward more satirical comedy, which has become the norm.
Today, French comedies still cultivate humour and popular
entertainment, but they also serve a social function:

As a genre comedy deliberately goes against the demands of realism ... yet it is perceived as serving a useful social and psychological function ... where repressed tensions can be released in a safe manner. (Hayward 1996: 55)

Influences and specificity of French contemporary comedy

Since the 1970s, French comedy has been influenced by Café-Théâtre cabaret tradition (e.g. troupes like 'Le Splendid' or 'Le Café de la Gare'). This tradition is based upon 'derision', i.e. making fun of serious matters, including 'self-derision' and satirical comments on society. These comedies are often based on loose plots (series of sketches or scenes), and break with the traditional image of star as hero.

Comedies are close to everyday life issues: family, relationships and crises, e.g. *Trois Hommes et un couffin/ Three Men and a Cradle* (1985); *La Crise* (1992); *Le Placard/ The Closet* (2001, 5.3M); *La Vie est un long fleuve tranquille/ Life is a Long Quiet River* (Chatiliez 1988); *Le Bonheur est dans le pré/ Happiness...* (Chatiliez 1995).

In the 1990s, French comedy has also been associated with an element of fantasy: *Delicatessen* (1990); *La Cité des enfants perdus/ The City of Lost Children* (1995); and *Les Visiteurs* (1993). While in the last ten years, comedy has brought into popular cinema a group of new comedians from innovative television channel Canal+, e.g. Antoine de Caunes, Les Nuls (Alain Chabat), José Garcia, Gad Elmaleh or Jamel Debbouze.

French comedy films are the most popular domestic films at the French box-office, but because of their cultural specificity, they tend to be confined to the national market and certain European countries (Francophone countries, Germany and Italy). Important examples of successful comedy classics over the years include:

- *Le Petit monde de Don Camillo* (1952, 12.8M).
- *La Grande vadrouille* (1966, record box-office hit 17M, not available in English).
- *Trois Hommes et un couffin* (10.2M), US remake: *Three men and a Baby* (1987).
- *Les Visiteurs* (13M and limited impact abroad), US remake: *Just Visiting* (2000).
- *Gazon Maudit/ French Twist* (1995, 3.9M).
- *Le Dîner de cons/ The Dinner Game* (1997, 10M and a good reception abroad).

- *Le Placard/ The Closet* (5.4M).
- *Astérix et Obélix: Mission Cléopâtre* (2002, 14.5M).
- *Chouchou* (2003, 3.7M).

'Film du look'

Definition

(See Austin 1996, Chapter 6)

The phrase 'film du look' has been created to define certain French films of the 1980s and early 1990s by three main directors: Luc Besson, Jean-Jacques Beineix and Leos Carax. It takes the form of a spectacular mainstream cinema directed at primarily young audiences, which displays specific forms of visual style and is influenced by other cinemas. The 'film du look' favours the visual and technical potential of cinema over the narrative, and demonstrates an explicit desire to make films for pleasure's sake, with a view to create 'trendy' spectacular entertainment.

Examples of 'films du look'

Directed by Beineix

- *Diva* (1981): First film du look, cult status, international impact, and a good example of postmodern cinema.
- *37'2 le matin/ Betty Blue* (1986): Cult film and considered by many as one of the most influential films of the decade.

Directed by Besson

- *Le Grand Bleu/ The Big Blue* (1988): Enormous popular success in France and abroad, cult status and considered by many as emblems of youth culture in the 1980s.
- *Nikita* (1989): International success and a US remake: *Point of No Return* (1993).
- *Léon* (1994): Worldwide success, released in two original sound versions, one in French and one in English.
- *Le Cinquième Elément/ The Fifth Element* (1997): International success, released in English language original version.
- *Jeanne d'Arc/Jeanne* (1999): Reasonable box-office success for a record budget French film, released in English language original version.

Directed by Carax

- *Les Amants du Pont-Neuf* (1991): A grand project as famous for its 'making-of' difficulties as for its spectacular originality.

These 'films du look' can be identified by a series of common characteristics:

1 Cartoon-like stereotyped young characters, who are not integrated into society and have communication problems.
2 Little emphasis on dialogue, which is mostly colloquial or even youth-related slang.
3 A semi-imaginary world, with a tension between the real and the ideal, and alienated urban surroundings.
4 A powerful visual style, combining bright colours, incongruous objects and artificial shots mixing realism and fantasy, old and new, nostalgia and modernity.
5 Numerous influences (pastiche and quotation) which are recycled (advertising world, Hollywood cinema, B-movies and popular culture more generally).
6 Combination of popular and high culture, and emphasis on art (transient fashion vs eternal art).

The 'films du look' marked the 1980s due to their national and international success at the box-office, which led to a 'cult cinema' status. The 'look' style continued to be influential in the 1990s, and it has often been related to other fantasy films, such as *Delicatessen*, a cult comedy which anticipates the style and originality of *Amélie*.

'Cinéma du look' has also been analysed as an illustration of postmodernist critical thought. However, it has had to withstand critical denigration campaigns in France where Besson and Beineix's films are generally considered as superficial commercial products, devoid of social content or message; in short, the antithesis of the French *auteur* tradition and a threat to the national identity of French cinema.

This section has highlighted the fluidity of the concept of genre, and it illustrates its potential national specificity. It also underlines the distinction between popular genres and *auteur* films in the perception of French cinema. The four genres mentioned here tend to be seen as popular genres in the French reception context, but they are often marketed as art cinema outside France.

CASE STUDY: *Le Fabuleux Destin d'Amélie Poulain/ Amélie* (Jeunet, 2001)

There are several reasons for selecting **Amélie** (the short GB/ US title is used for convenience) as the second case study covering contemporary French cinema. The film is a recent and accessible example of popular French cinema, which had an exceptional public and critical reception in France and abroad. The case study discusses aspects of genre, representation of identity, narrative, style and aesthetic approach, and finally reception. The film can be used to illustrate general filmic issues, or for close study purposes. It also lends itself to a comparative study with **Les 400 Coups**, especially since Jeunet recognised Truffaut's film as a source of inspiration.

Jean-Pierre Jeunet

Jean-Pierre Jeunet was born in Roanne, France in 1955. Self-taught, he started as a director by shooting television commercials, music videos and short films.

An admirer of the works of Tex Avery, Jean-Pierre Jeunet is a passionate follower of comics and cartoons. He began his career directing two animated short films with Marc Caro: **L'Évasion/ The Escape** (1978) and **Le Manège/ The Merry-go-round** (1980). For **Le Bunker de la Dernière Rafale/ The Last Burst Bunker** (1981), Jeunet and Caro constructed the army and the costumes, down to the smallest details, in a year. In 1985, his short film **Pas de repos pour Billy Brakko** received many awards on the film festival circuit. **Foutaises** (1989), his last short to date, was also well received.

Jeunet launched his feature film career and established himself as a film-maker, with the international hit comedy **Delicatessen**, co-written and co-directed with Caro. The film received countless awards.

Jeunet continued his success with the critically acclaimed film **La Cité des Enfants Perdus /The City of Lost Children**, a superb dark and poetic fable, which was a Cannes Film Festival Official Selection and nominated by Independent Spirit Awards as best foreign film. He was then asked by 20th Century Fox to shoot the fourth episode of the Alien saga, **Alien: Resurrection** (1997), after which he returned to France to start **Amélie**.

Following the world success of the film, he went on to direct **A Very Long Engagement** (2004), an ambitious project produced by Warner Bros but shot in France with a French technical team and French cast. The film, designed to become a blockbuster distributed worldwide, was at the centre of a controversy over its nationality and did not quite repeat the success of **Amélie** (4,5M spectators in France).

The film

Jeunet sees **Amélie** as his most personal film, having had it in mind for 25 years. **Foutaises**, his short film of 1989 featuring Dominique Pinon, was a first attempt at putting into pictures some of the formal and thematic ideas developed in **Amélie**. The actual starting point of the Amélie project, however, was a small notebook in which he recorded ideas, stories, memories and anecdotes. After developing the concept and main character, the screenplay was co-written with Guillaume Laurant.

Jeunet has clearly commented upon his intentions in numerous interviews that he gave about the film (see DVD interview for example): he wanted to move away from some of the naturalistic New Wave values and the social realism of the 1990s, and film a positive and generous story, with a playful approach to film-making using visual aesthetics. He also wanted to make a personal film with artistic freedom after the constrictive experience of Hollywood production practice during **Alien: Resurrection**. The result is a film which is both

Biographical note adapted from www.frenchcul ture.org/cinem a/festival/jeune t/index.html

surreal and anchored in the real world. It is influenced by different elements of French cinema's heritage, namely Jacques Prévert's sense of dialogue and Marcel Carné's poetic realism, Truffaut's representation of Paris, and aspects of the visual style of the 1980s and links with his previous films with Marc Caro.

Synopsis

Amélie is first presented as a charming little girl brought up by unconventional parents in Paris in the 1980s. As a young woman, she comes to live in a small flat in Montmartre where she finds work in a local cafe. One evening in 1997, she finds an old box full of a child's treasures behind her bathroom wall, and she sets out to find this child (now a man in his forties) in order to return the box. This enables her to get to know her neighbours better, and to realise that they all seem to have problems that make them unhappy. She also meets a young man who collects abandoned identity photographs found all around Paris. She falls in love with him instantly and tries to meet him again, while at the same time devising a series of convoluted plans designed to make her new friends happier.

Genre

In terms of genre and identity, *Amélie* combines a number of influences, such as (1) the legacy of French popular cinema tradition and the 'poetic realism' of Renoir or Carné which goes back to the 1930s, and which can be related to the 'magical realism' of more recent world literature; (2) the *auteurist* values of personal artistic creation; and (3) the popular visual style associated with advertising and 'film du look' in the 1980s.

Jeunet also represents a generation of directors of the 1990s who can offer a popular alternative to Hollywood cinema, and the success of *Amélie* illustrates the vitality of French cinema in the 2000s, in spite of concern over its future.

The film lends itself well to a genre study, as it combines universal conventions with typically French genre influences, which contribute to a sense of originality and national identity. The film is often described as a romantic comedy with a feel-good factor and traditional quest for love and happiness. It comprises an element of melodrama, and focuses on generating nostalgia, emotion and personal identification. It also appropriates some conventions attached to the (fairy) tale. But what distinguishes *Amélie* from these familiar genres is the use of magical realism conventions, which draw away from objective representation and enrich a realistic use of details with elements of fantasy and a surreal way of portraying emotion. As a result, the film is not meant to be taken too literally, more as a fable with its symbolic and metaphoric structure, and a new way of perceiving the world, through a child's eyes for instance.

The visual style and use of new digital technology point at Jeunet's own artistic signature, and the success of the film can be partly attributed to his 'ability to present his nostalgic vision through high tech mise-en-scène and aesthetics drawn from cartoons and commercials' (Vincendeau 2001). Genre mixing is a characteristic of the film, reminiscent of the 'film du look' practices, and *Amélie* can also be read using the framework of postmodernist film theory.

Narrative

In keeping with the fairytale conventions, the narrative is linear and resorts to an omniscient narrator (Dussolier) who sets the scene for the first 20 minutes of the film. Only then does Amélie take over the narrative, and start living and speaking even though the narrator still intervenes regularly to comment upon the action. The description of Amélie's childhood is presented as a flashback, and it functions as an explanation for her adult personality.

The editing of the film is an important feature. It is fast cut and intricate, and it contributes to the surreal atmosphere of the film with ellipses and surprise effects. The post-production was particularly innovative: it used digital technology to improve the film's visual style, with stunning special effects. colour grading and non-linear editing, in collaboration with the reputed French post-production company Duboi.

The film's plot develops loosely around a number of self-standing episodes and sub-plots, which introduce a gallery of atypical secondary characters (Amélie's father, Raymond Dufayel the painter, Georgette the hypochondriac, Madame Wallace the concierge, Bretodeau, Collignon, the grocer and his assistant Lucien). The only link between them is Amélie, around whom the film is constructed.

Constructing characters: The case of Amélie

A character is usually constructed using two different approaches:

1 It is defined in terms of the characteristics, which are attributed to the hero/heroine. These include the personal information on the character (age, class, profession, gender, power relationship with others, etc.) and narrative information (response to specific situations, e.g. when and where the character appears, how often, in what circumstances, etc.).

2 It is marked by traits, which differentiate the hero/heroine from the others.

In the case of *Amélie*, the spectator is a witness to the conception of the main character Amélie, and is given a lengthy account of her childhood, using the voice-over and flashback techniques. The spectator is informed on her origins, her family background, her routine, likes and dislikes, fears and dreams, using a strategy later reproduced more concisely for the other protagonists.

Amélie's character combines the three typical aspects of the romantic heroine: a **narrative principle** by which the other characters are arranged around the main protagonist; a **projection principle** whereby the spectator identifies with her (see reviews) and an **ideological principle** which supports the values of the protagonist (or of the auteur of the film). In the case of Amélie, the spectator identifies with the innocence of the lonely young woman, her attempts to help others and her quest for happiness.

There are different ways to approach the character study of Amélie (and similarly of the other characters of the film if relevant), as good or bad, active or passive, conformist or outsider, liar or impostor, strong or weak personality, relationship with others, etc.

Moreover, characters may change through the development of the narrative. Amélie's personality evolves as the story unfolds. The first turning point of the film is the discovery of the treasure-box, which leads to the decision to improve the lives of the people around her. It may therefore be useful to analyse the evolution of the character -her fears and aspirations, her schemes and her refusal to face her destiny. It will show that her trajectory is an ascending one, as is conventional for comedy heroines (in a tragedy, it is often a process of decline climaxing with an unhappy ending).

Character transformation is an important aspect of dramatic development of the narrative as well as a vehicle for in-depth characterisation. In Amélie's case, it takes the form of a rite of passage, a coming of age, from child to adult, from dreamland to the real world. (See also Antoine Doinel in *Les 400 Coups* for comparison purposes.)

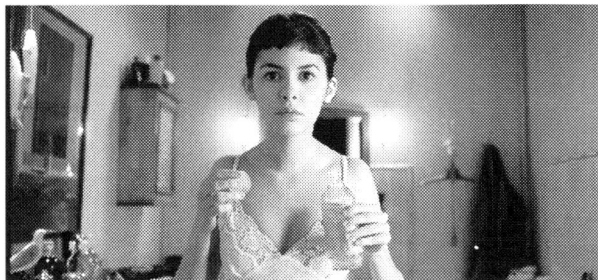

© BFI Stills

Main themes and style

When watching a French film, English students may be attracted to, or put off by, the foreignness of the characters, settings, dialogue and cultural values. The thematic input of the film will also affect their perception of national identity.

The film *Amélie* does not really have any French social-realist aspirations, yet the reviews in France and Britain tend to refer to its themes in their French cultural context, and to associate the success of the film with a 'social phenomenon'. Yet, *Amélie* contains few references to the France of 1997 in which the film is set, except the death of Princess Diana, but it resorts to a number of French stereotypes mostly linked to a romantic and exotic vision of France, and a nostalgic representation of Paris. These stereotypes are combined with an ideal of romantic love, a sense of adventure and quest, and a more diffuse impression of style. The musical score, composed by Yann Tiersen, features accordion and waltz, and enhances the romantic love theme, symbolised by the recurrent red colour tones, secret notes, messages, flowers, dreams and mystery. Amélie craves for true love and chases the romantic stereotype of the young heroic 'charming prince' in the form of the mysterious Nino Quincampoix.

The film promotes an idealised retro representation of Paris, as a colourful space of wonder and mystery. With its tourist attractions, monuments and historical heritage, Montmartre is presented as a picturesque artist area. Jeunet said that he wanted every frame to look like a painting. Although the exterior scenes are mostly shot on location, many shots have been touched up digitally in post-production (e.g. matte painting and manipulation of colour, such as cloud effects on dull skies, or enhanced colours in the underground or indoors). Cars, rubbish and graffiti have been deleted. Paris is portrayed as a clean, non-threatening city, promoting a social atmosphere in which cafes are lively and convivial, and public places gradually become social points (fairground, metro, street, station and Sacré-Coeur). It is a privileged setting for adventure, mystery, imagination and fantasy (chases, hide-and-seek games, dramatised situations). Paris plays an important part in the film, and students may wish to compare the representation of the city in **Amélie** with that of other French films (Trauner's sets and the poetic realism of the 1930s, the Paris of the New Wave or the underground atmosphere of 'films du look', etc.).

The film encourages nostalgia, with posters, images and carefully chosen objects of reference that spectators can identify with and relate to their own experience: 'crème brûlée', garden dwarfs, old love letters, card collections, toys, familiar Renoir paintings, black and white 'stock shoots' of the Tour de France cycle race, accordion music. As such, the film offers a traditional, quirky representation of France before the globalisation era with no mention of Hollywood, no Internet, no McDonald's, even if paradoxically, Jeunet uses high-tech film technology to achieve his unique timeless style.

It appears from discussions about his films (e.g. interviews or **Amélie**'s DVD commentary) that Jeunet's style is a product of different influences: science fiction, animation, advertising French poetic realism and American cinema. His trademark since **Delicatessen** and **Alien: Resurrection** has been a unique visual style, focusing on beautiful images, carefully designed at the writing stage (use of storyboards) and before shooting (camcorder trials, freeze-frames and rehearsals with the actors).

Jeunet's style produces an effect of surprise. It transforms everyday events and objects into compelling images, in which the influence of advertising and animation films is perceptible. The digital editing techniques used and the extended post-production work also play significant parts in the end result. The 123 digital visual special effects created by the Duboi studio (the rabbit shaped cloud, the heartbeat, the key in the pocket, the animated painting, etc.), and the various 'corrections' including enhanced colours and deletion of unwanted objects, prevent a strictly naturalist reading of the film.

Study of individual scenes
Key Scene 1: The discovery of the box
(DVD chapter 5)

This is a key scene from a narrative viewpoint, as it changes the course of Amélie's life.

Context: Just after hearing of the death of Princess Diana on television, which is the only temporal marker of the film locating the plot in 1997, Amélie inadvertently discovers a box full of childhood treasures dating from the 1950s in a cavity of her bathroom wall. Nostalgic for her own childhood, she decides to return it to its owner and starts an investigation, which she sees as a challenge.

Narrative: The scene is narrated in voice-over, adopting an omniscient viewpoint. Amélie remains silent, but the narrator interprets her actions and reactions, and highlights the scene as the turning point in her life.

Style: The scene illustrates the stylistic characteristics of the film discussed above: the retro décor of Amélie's flat with red and green as dominant colour schemes, and the special attention given to objects and detail (the TV set, the bath).

Amélie is central to the plot and narrative, and the camera focuses on her. It follows her. The use of a wide-angle lens, close-up and the zoom in are recurrent motifs, which convey Amélie's emotions (here surprise). The accordion musical theme illustrates her decision to find the owner of the box, and later in the film, it underlines the success of one of her plans.

The sound effects are also carefully chosen to create dramatic effects: the round perfume cap rolling on the bathroom tiles; the fantastic, mysterious atmosphere as she discovers the box is enhanced by conspicuous sound and artificial lighting effects.

Amélie suddenly has a strange feeling

Key Scene 2: The blind man's trip (DVD chapter 5)
This scene illustrates different aspects of Jeunet's original visual style.

Context: A happy Amélie walks in a postcard-like Paris, having returned the box to Bretodeau and seen the emotional effect of her trick. This accomplishment fills her with 'a strange feeling of absolute harmony' and 'an urge to help mankind'. She starts by helping a blind man cross the street and make his way to the underground, while she describes for him the beauty and quaintness of a busy Paris street.

Narrative: This scene is a good example of the digressions punctuating the narrative of *Amélie*. It does not have any other function than to enhance a visual pleasure with a verbal commentary. It is the first time that the shy and withdrawn Amélie expresses herself so uninhibitedly.

Style: The scene illustrates the idealised retro representation of Paris. The lighting is soft to show that Amélie is in harmony with the city. Amélie is shot in profile using a steadycam as she walks over a bridge, the slow-motion and camera movement emphasise her light-hearted mood and the liveliness that she communicates. Conversely, the brisk camera movements, as Amélie describes the street to the blind man, place the emphasis of precise objects or vignettes in which quaintness is more important than realism.

Editing: Using the techniques of advertising and music video, the scene is cut fast, changing the focus of attention rapidly, thereby accelerating the pace of the action and manipulating what the spectator perceives on screen.

The editing and camera work recreate the metaphor of a ride on a merry-go-round, in which the rider is transported for 30 seconds into another world, that of people who can see. For the blind man it is an imagined world, for the audience it can appear exotic or evoke nostalgic memories.

Use of space: Jeunet says that he likes to place the camera near the ground, and as often in the film, we see the blind man's feet before the camera moves up to his face. The stairs of the underground provide an opportunity for an aesthetic location shot using a vertical camera movement.

Special effects: A flash of light coming from above envelops the blind man to convey the warmth and liveliness that he felt for a few seconds. He has been included into the life of those whom he cannot see and their small daily pleasures.

Sound effects: The fast moving camera is often accompanied by a rustling sound, reminiscent of cartoons. The familiar accordion theme related to Amélie and Paris indicates that she has just successfully performed a good deed. It serves as a form of punctuation.

Key Scene 3: The kiss and the last scene (DVD chapter 16)

Context: Having just watched the video of Dufayel the painter, Amélie realises that she must find Nino and, as she opens the door, there he stands. They kiss... The film ends with the resolution of a number of secondary plots, and with Nino and Amélie riding through Paris on Nino's scooter.

Narrative: The epilogue of the film provides an unambiguous closure of happy ending, which is in keeping with popular cinema and fairytale conventions. Four short scenes summarise the happy resolution of the various sub-plots. The final scooter scene as they tour round Paris is briskly edited. Even the voice-over narrator seems over-precise and redundant.

Style: The slow scene of the kiss is a silent one shot in close-up. It places the emphasis on romantic love and contrasts with the accelerated motion of the last scene, which promotes movement, freedom and new beginnings.

The film ends on a last emblematic object: the marshmallow machine is twisting its pink paste and creating a hypnotising effect on the spectator, and acts as a metaphor for the utopian and escapist nature of the film.

Marketing and reception

Amélie can be used as an example of both commercial and critical success, which illustrates the marketing and distribution of non-Hollywood films, and other related reception issues. *Amélie* was a huge box-office success in 2001, with more than 30 million spectators worldwide, and 8.6 million in France alone (on 432 screens). Nevertheless, the financing of the film had proved difficult in spite of Jeunet's experience. Seventy-seven million francs were needed (just 10% of the budget of *Alien:*

Significantly,
the French film
industry still
tends to
calculate film
receipts in
terms of
number of
spectators in
cinemas rather
than gross
takings and
profits.

Resurrection), and several companies rejected the film before UGC agreed to produce, manage the international rights and distribute it. **Amélie** opened in France in April 2001, partly because it had not been selected for the Cannes Festival. This was denounced retrospectively and used by some to illustrate what they believed was an elitist policy of this important international institution.

Following the film's success in France, Momentum distributed the film in Britain where it was released in October on 82 screens and a hefty publicity campaign of £600,000 (sponsored by a brand of French liqueur!). One million spectators saw the film and it received two BAFTA awards. It was then released in America by Miramax in November 2001 – a few months after the events on 11 September – attracting a French language film record 3M spectators and receipts of $20M. The film was nominated for five Academy Awards, which resulted in substantial media exposure and an extended presence on cinema screens.

The surprise success of **Amélie** in France has been interpreted in different ways. Initially, the film received mostly positive reviews, and attracted record numbers of spectators in the first weeks. It became a cinematic event, a symbol of the renewed vitality of French cinema in the context of pessimistic predictions regarding its future as a viable industry at the end of the twentieth century.

Amélie also became a social phenomenon, in keeping with the French public's expectations and state of mind. It translated a feel-good factor into images, and promoted traditional values of happiness, sense of community, family and true love, values often considered old fashioned and nostalgic in today's French cinematic context. **Amélie's** values were even appropriated by the French politicians for the presidential campaign of 2002: President Jacques Chirac organised a screening at the Elysée Palace, and Prime Minister Lionel Jospin showed the film to his cabinet, generating extensive political comments in the media.

The film received a great deal of media attention in France, and its reception exceeded the cinema sphere as it became the centre of:

1   A critical and intellectual debate initiated by the respected but elitist French cultural magazine 'Les Inrockuptibles', which accused **Amélie** of offering an unrealistic and simplistic vision of Montmartre, and a

representation of Paris which erased the cultural and ethnic diversity and could almost be associated with National Front values.

2 A society and cultural debate comparing cinema and reality TV. *Amélie* was released in France at the same time as the first reality television show *Loft Story*, the French equivalent of *Big Brother*, and was surrounded by three months of heated controversy and intense media coverage, in which on several occasions *Amélie* and *Loft Story* were compared and analysed together.

The reception of *Amélie* abroad highlighted the *Frenchness* of the film, its foreignness, exotic and unfamiliar feel, which were all marketing assets and contributed to its success. The international impact was probably enhanced by the need for escapist entertainment away from the real world events of September 2001.

It may be useful to carry out a detailed study of the UK or US reception of the film to examine questions related to the perception of Frenchness and the elements that contribute to the construction of the film's national identity.

Conclusion: French Cinema, Hollywood and 'Cultural Exception'

This introduction to French cinema as an example of non-Hollywood cinema has been aimed at presenting some specific aspects of French film production that are relevant for Film Studies students, such as its historical legacy, its relationship with genre or its national identity. It also raises, however briefly, a number of related issues, including the relevance today of adopting an *auteur* approach to cinema, the specificity of the French film industry, and the dichotomy between artistic pursuit and popular success.

The debate around French cinema in the last decade has tended to concentrate on the notion of 'cultural exception', which is worth exploring briefly in conclusion, as it epitomises the possible problems facing French cinema at the dawn of the twenty-first century.

Over the years, cinema has had a specific place in European cultures. In brief, it was aimed at a certain elite and generated by this elite. As a result, European cinemas were eager to preserve their national character, while they were increasingly confronted by the domination of Hollywood cinema, which conversely was aimed at a wide popular audience.

To counteract this, the EU countries, and particularly France, which has the most substantial film industry, have put in place over the years a series of measures, which can be considered as protectionist, and which aim at ensuring the survival of a vital economic and cultural sector. These include a number of government subsidies to the film industry, and the imposition of quotas on the national TV channels. In 1993, the US government tried to have these measures abolished in the name of the international free trade agreements, which in turn led to strong opposition from the EU with France at the forefront. It is in the context of this conflict that the term 'cultural exception' became central to the public debate in France. Because of the excluding connotation of the term it was then replaced by the more positive term of 'cultural diversity' (Lalumière 2000).

What was initially a political conflict soon changed into a general public debate with strong reactions from a number of intellectuals, the French press, many cinema and television personalities (e.g. Bertrand Tavernier, Jean-Jacques Beineix), and from the public more generally. It led to the GATT Agreements, which left the audiovisual products out of the system, which implies that the following measures continue to apply in France (Regourd 2002: 32-48):

1 **Financial support** (compte de soutien) to the production of French films funded from three main sources: a tax on cinema admissions (since 1959); a tax on television receipts (since 1984, it brings 70% of the total income); and a tax on video tapes (since 1992).
2 **TV co-production**: television channels have to devote 3.2% of their turnover to produce French films.
3 **Television quotas**: 60% of films broadcast on French channels must be allocated to original French productions.
4 The European directive 'television without borders' also establishes quotas for European films (1989 revised in 1997).

The French film industry needs to address a number of issues in the near future, if it is to remain a force to be reckoned with in the increasingly globalised market of cinema. The stakes are enormous because the audiovisual industry in France represents huge economical interest but it also supports the film production system. One important challenge will be to ensure the continuation of a system in which *auteur* films, which contribute substantially to the French cinema identity, can exist alongside more popular, commercially viable ventures. Another challenge concerns the financing of films, and depends partly on the uncertain future of Canal+, which until 2001 represented a major financial input for the French film industry. Finally, the most difficult challenge for French cinema is to continue to be internationally renowned, while retaining its identity.

Sample Questions

(Elements of answers in italics.)

- **To what extent do New Wave values still affect our perception of French cinema?**
  Auteur *approach in contemporary French cinema; accent on director-based film analysis; the personal thematic lines; the continued careers of New Wave actors and directors to the present; the legacy of New Wave films as inspiration and influence for some new young directors of 1980s-1990s (e.g. Carax, Depleschin, Assayas).*

- **Discuss the personal element in New Wave cinema.** *(See New Wave, Section 2 above.)*

- **Compare the role played by the director in French cinema and in Hollywood.**
  This essay focuses on the role of director in the French film production and distribution system, and may include an analysis of film-maker as auteur, who as well as director, may also be the scriptwriter, producer, actor, casting director of his/her film (e.g. Truffaut, Jeunet, Kassovitz, Coline Serreau, Josiane Balasko or Woody Allen). Even the more popular film-makers in the 'tradition de qualité' or comedies tend to have more control over the film in the French system than in Hollywood (e.g. Jean-Marie Poiré, Patrice Leconte, Claude Berri). They also contribute actively to the promotion campaigns in France and abroad.

- **Discuss the foreign spectator's possible responses to a French heritage film.**
  This question focuses on the spectator's experience of the spectacular and access to other cultures through cinema; sensation of foreignness and exoticism; contrasting with Hollywood familiar cinema genres, narratives and styles (e.g. **La Reine Margot, Amélie, Lucie Aubrac,** *etc.).*

- **To what extent can 'film du look' be considered as France's response to Hollywood blockbusters?**
  Analysis of main similarities and differences in terms of

production values, themes, visual style and target audience.
- **Analyse the specificity of the film industry in France in the 1980s and 1990s.**
  Analysis of Lang's cultural policy; co-existence of different popular genres ('film du look', heritage, intimist, comedy), and an auteur cinema relying on state subsidy.
- **To what extent is 'Frenchness' a marketing device for French cinema abroad?**
  Answers should include different perspectives, such as language, geographical surroundings, stars and other relevant aspects of national identity.
- **Is genre a major element in the construction of French cinema's image abroad?**
  In short, yes. Heritage and intimist genres could be used as case studies to illustrate patterns of familiarity and difference, enabling French cinema to construct its identity abroad. Stars and language are other contributing factors.

Further analysis and possible essay/discussion questions on *Amélie*

(Elements of answer in case study)

1. To what extent does *Amélie* draw upon the French New Wave values?
2. Analyse *Amélie* from a genre perspective.
3. Does *Amélie* illustrate the evolution of the popular 'film du look' of the 1980s?
4. To what extent is *Amélie*'s success abroad representative of French cinema's international scope?

Further analysis and possible essay/discussion questions on *Les 400 Coups*

(Elements of answer in case study)

1. What main Truffaut themes are already present in *Les 400 Coups?*
2. To what extent does *Les 400 Coups* epitomise the style of the French New Wave?
3. How do Truffaut's films reflect his personal experience? To what extent is Antoine Doinel/ Jean-Pierre Léaud the alter-ego of the director?
4. Analyse the relationship of Antoine Doinel with the adults in the film.
5. How are women represented in *Les 400 Coups?*

6. Analyse the treatment of space in *Les 400 Coups*.

Select Filmography

Here are a few films representative of French cinema that are available in VHS/DVD and could be used in class as illustrations or case studies.

Film	Synopsis	Teaching interest	Video/ DVD
Les 400 coups (Truffaut 1959)	A young teenager ends up in a youth detention centre after discovering how hard it is to grow up. New Wave themes and style.	A major classic.	VHS/ DVD (Subs)
A Bout de souffle (Godard 1959)	A young criminal arrives in Paris and meets an American girl who betrays him. New Wave style and innovative editing.	Character study of Michel Poiccard.	VHS/ DVD (Subs)
Jean de Florette (Berri 1985)	A city man and his family arrive in a Provence farm that they have inherited but they can't find the source which would help them to survive.	Heritage film. French production values, international success and issues of national identity.	VHS/ DVD (Subs)

Le Grand Bleu (Besson 1988)	A young diver competes for a world record and has to choose between a woman and a dolphin.	Film as visual entertainment. Cult film of 1980s generation.	VHS/ DVD (Subs + English Version)
Cyrano de Bergerac (Rappeneau 1989)	Romantic tragedy about a 17th c. nobleman who believes he is too ugly because of his grotesque nose to ever win Roxane and helps Christian, a tongue-tied soldier, to woo her with love letters.	Cultural heritage and literary adaptation of a classic play.	VHS/ DVD (Subs)
Delicatessen (Jeunet and Caro 1990)	In a wartime context of famine, a young artist comes to live in the top floor of a strange house where finding meat seems to be easy.	Cult black comedy. French cinema as different 'other'.	VHS/ DVD (Subs)
Nikita (Besson 1990)	A female drug addict is imprisoned after killing a policeman. She is offered a deal to save her life by the secret services and trains to become a professional killer. 'Film du look' genre.	Developing international production values. Luc Besson's place in French cinema.	VHS/ DVD (Subs)
Les Visiteurs (Poiré 1993)	A medieval Count and his servant land into the twentieth century and discover the changes that have taken place in the last millennium.	Light class comedy based on French historical heritage. Use of language and national identity.	VHS/ DVD (Subs)

La **Cérémonie** (Chabrol 1995)	A young woman comes to work as a housekeeper for a bourgeois family in Brittany	The evolution of a New Wave director into a master of the French style thriller.	VHS/ DVD (Subs)
Chacun **cherche** *son chat* (Klapisch 1995)	A young woman living in Paris district has lost her cat and while looking for it she discovers the charm of the area and the people living there. Poetic realism and 'intimist' values.	Representation of Paris.	VHS (Subs)
Gazon **Maudit** (Balasko 1995)	A housewife falls in love with a butch lesbian, and upsets the family routine of her philandering and homophobic husband. Comedy of mores.	Gender issues.	VHS/ DVD (Subs)
La Haine (Kassovitz 1995)	A day in the life of three aimless youths from a deprived Paris suburb.	Banlieue film, youth film and controversial representation of French cultural diversity.	VHS/ DVD (Subs)
Lucie **Aubrac** (Berri 1996)	Resistance drama based on a true story relating to the arrest of Jean Moulin and the escape of fellow resistant Raymond Aubrac thanks to the determination of wife Lucie. Heritage film production values. More emphasis on love story than on historical background.	National identity and use of stars.	VHS (Subs)

Le Dîner de cons (Veber 1997)	A middle class group of friends organise weekly dinners where they invite and make fun of an 'idiot' who is not aware of the situation. But this week's idiot might surprise them. Comedy of mores derived from a successful play.	Character study. Comedy conventions.	VHS/ DVD (Subs)
Le Placard (Veber 2000)	A man learns that he is about to be sacked and finds a way to keep his job using social prejudice and political correctness to his advantage.	Mainstream social comedy with a tolerance and gender agenda.	VHS/ DVD (Subs)
Les Rivières pourpres (Kassovitz 2000)	Two different police officers meet while investigating a bizarre murder near a legendary private school isolated in the Alps.	Thriller conventions and action give this French genre film a Hollywood feel and an international scope.	VHS/ DVD (Subs + English Version)
Être et avoir (Philibert 2001)	6 months of the life of a rural primary school in rural Auvergne. Documentary genre and style.	Non-professional actors, focus on realism.	VHS/ DVD (Subs)
Le fabuleux Destin d'Amélie Poulain (Jeunet 2001)	A young woman decides to make other people happy and change their lives, but is afraid of living her own life. Poetic fantasy and technological innovation.	French stereotypes. Audience study. (See case study.)	VHS/ DVD (Subs)

Huit Femmes / 8 Women (Ozon 2002)	8 women are trapped in an isolated house after a murder and they all have something to hide. Comedy.	Visual style and influence of Hollywood.	VHS/ DVD (Subs)
L'Auberge espagnole/ Pot Luck (Klapisch 2003)	A French student on an Erasmus exchange shares a flat in Barcelona with other European flatmates. Comedy. National stereotypes.	Towards a form of European cinema.	VHS/ DVD (Subs)
Les Choristes (Barratier 2004)	In 1949 a new music teacher arrives in a rural boarding school for boys and starts a new choir. Intimist period drama.	Representation of rural France and education. Social phenomenon in France (audience study).	VHS/ DVD (Subs)

Select Bibliography

GENERAL REFERENCE

- Austin, G. *French Contemporary Cinema*. Manchester: MUP, 1996.
  Main recommended source of reference for teachers and students. Excellent introduction to French cinema (genre approach and individual studies of contemporary films).
- Powrie, P. and Reader, K. *French Cinema: A Students Guide*. Oxford: Arnold, 2002.
  Recommended resource book on French cinema as an academic subject, with chapters devoted to historical,

theoretical and critical issues, as well as essay samples
and analyses of film sequences.

- Vincendeau, G. *The Companion to French Cinema*.
London: Cassell, 1996.
Alphabetical entries on directors and actors, and
definition of key notions in French cinema.

- Temple.M. and Witt, M. *The French Cinema Book*.
London: BFI, 2004.
Insights into a variety of key issues about French cinema
covering different periods.

SPECIFIC PERIODS

- Andrew, D. *Mist of Regret. Culture and Sensibility in
Classic French Film*. Princeton: Princeton University
Press, 1995.

- Crisp, C. *The Classic French Cinema, 1930-1960*.
Bloomington: Indiana University Press, 1997.

- Lanzoni, R. *French Cinema: From its Beginnings to
the Present* London: Continuum, 2002.

- Wilson, E. *French Cinema since 1950*. London:
Duckworth, 1999.

NEW WAVE

- Andrew, D. *André Bazin*. Oxford: Oxford University
Press, 1978; New York: Columbia University Press, 1990.

- Bazin, A. *What is Cinema?* Trans. H. Gray, Berkeley:
University of California Press, 1958.

- Bordwell, D.and Thompsen, K. *Film Art: An
Introduction*. New York: McGraw-Hill, 1993: 479-83.

- Caughie, J. *Theories of Authorship*. London: Routledge,
1981.

- Caughie, J. 'Teaching through Authorship' *The Screen
Education Reader*. London: MacMillan, 1993.

- Douchet, J. '*The French New Wave: Its Influence and
Decline*' Cineaste 24.1 (1998): 16-18.

- Douchet, J. *French New Wave*. Trans. R. Bononno,
DPA/editions Hazan, 2000.

- Hillier, J. *Cahiers du cinéma* - Vol. 1: 1950s. London:
Routledge in association with the British Film Institute,
1985.

- Hillier, J. *Cahiers du cinéma* - Vol. 2: 1960-1968.
Cambridge, Mass.: Harvard University Press, 1986.

- Monaco, J. *The New Wave*. New York: Oxford University Press, 1976.
- Wiegand, C. *The New Wave*. Harpenden: Pocket Essentials, 2001.
  Useful introductory account of the New Wave including individual presentation of all major films of the period. Recommended for student use.

ON TRUFFAUT AND *LES 400 COUPS*
- De Baecque, A. and Toubiana, S. *François Truffaut*. Trans. C. Temerson, New York: Knopf, 1999.
- Gillain, A. *Les 400 Coups*. Paris: Nathan, 1991.
- Gillain, A. '*The Script of Deliquency: François Truffaut's Les 400 Coups*' in Hayward and Vincendeau (2000).
- Holmes, D. and Ingram, R. *François Truffaut*. Manchester: Manchester University Press, 1998.
- Insdorf, A. *François Truffaut*. Cambridge: Cambridge University Press, 1994.
- Nicholls, D. *François Truffaut* London: Batsford, 1993.
- Raskin, R. '*A Note on Closure in Truffaut's Les 400 Coups*'
  http://imv.au.dk/publikationer/pov/Issue_02/section_3/artc3B.html#fn1
- Truffaut, F. *The Films in my Life*. Trans. L. Mayhew, New York: Da Capo, 1994.

STUDIES OF CONTEMPORARY FRENCH FILMS
- Boorman, J. and Donohue, W. (eds) *Projections 9 French: Film-makers on Film-making*. London: Faber and Faber, 1999.
- Darke, C. *Light Readings*. London: Wallflower, 2000.
- Hayward, S. and Vincendeau, G. (eds) *French Films: Texts and Contexts*. Second edition, London: Routledge, 2000.
- Mazdon, L. (ed.) *France on Film*. London: Wallflower, 2000.
- Powrie, P. *French Cinema in the 1980s: The Crisis of Masculinity*. Manchester: Manchester University Press, 1997.
- Powrie, P. *French Cinema in the 1990s: Continuity and Change*. Manchester: Manchester University Press, 1999.

- Stafford, R. *La Haine/ Hate*. York study notes, 1999.

NATIONAL IDENTITY
- Buss, R. *The French through their Films*. London, 1988.
- Ezra, E. and Harris, S. *France in Focus. Film and National Identity*. Oxford: Berg, 2000.
- Forbes, J. *The Cinema in France after the New Wave*. London: Macmillan, 1992.
- Forbes, J. *'Keeping it in the Family' Sight and Sound* May 1994: 24-6.
- Hayward, S. *French National Cinema*. London: Routledge, 1993.
- Lalumière, C. (2000) *'The Battle of Cultural Diversity'* Label France January 2000 http://www.france.diplomatie.fr/label_france/ENGLISH/DOSSIER/2000/10culturelle.html
- Liehm, R. (1996) *'The Cultural exception: Why?'*
- http://www.arts.uwaterloo.ca/FINE/juhde/liehm962.htm
- Mazdon, L. Encore *Hollywood: Remaking French Cinema*, London: BFI, 2000.
- Regourd, S. *L'Exception culturelle*, Paris: PUF, 2002.
- Tartaglione, N. *'Claude Berri Simply the best'* Interview http://www.filmfestivals.com/cannes98/homaus2.htm

ON *AMÉLIE*
- 'Amélie', *Film Journal International* 28 August 2002.
- Dawson, J. 'Lie Back and Think of France' *Times* 14 October 2001: 10-11.
- Edwards, R. 'Interview with Jeunet' *Empire* http://www.empireonline.co.uk/features/interviews/Amélie
- Ellen, B. 'A Spoonful of sugar...' *Times* 4 October 2001: 11-13.
- Jeffries, S. 'The French Insurrection' *Observer* 24 June 2001.
- Johnston, S. 'A French Fairy Tale' October 2001: 40-2. *Times*
- Jeffries, S. 'Here's Looking at You, Kid' *Guardian* 2 October 2001: 14-15.
- Kempley, R. 'Amélie: Candy-Coated, Magically Delicious'

Washington Post 9 November 2001: 5.
- Landesman, C. 'Joie de Vivre' *Times* 7 October 2001: 8.
- Meyer, A. 'The Fabulous Destiny of Jean-Pierre Jeunet', *Indie Wire*, November 2002 http://www.indiewire.com/film/interviews/int_jeunet_jea npier_011102.html
- Mitchell, E. 'Little Miss Sunshine as Urban Sprite' *New York Times* 2 November 2001.
- Nesselson, L. 'Amélie from Montmartre' *Variety* 30 April 2001: 26.
- O'Hagan, A. 'Princess Charming' *Daily Telegraph* 5 October 2001: 27.
- O'Sullivan, C. 'Amélie' *Sight and Sound* October 2001: 40-1.
- Potton, E. 'Gallic Crush' *Times* 6 October 2001:7.
- Preston, P. 'Soft Choux Shuffle' *Guardian* 7 October 2001.
- Quinn, A. 'The Big Picture: Amélie' *Independent* 5 October 2001.
- Steinberg, S. 'The Thoroughly Conformist World of Amélie' *World Socialist Web* www.wsws.org 28 August 2001.
- Vincendeau, G. 'Café Society' *Sight and Sound* August 2002 http://www.bfi.org.uk/sightandsound/2001_08/ cafesociety.html

OTHER USEFUL WORKS
- Corrigan, T. *A Short Guide to Writing about Film*. New York: Harper Collins, 1994.
- Hayward, S. *Key Concepts in Cinema Sudies*. London: Routledge, 1996 and 2000.
  These last two books provide detailed critical definitions of key concepts used in this section although they are not specifically on French cinema.

For statistics and information of the French film industry, the CNC publications (12 Rue de Lubeck, 75784 Paris Cedex 16 or www.cnc.fr) are very useful sources of information also available in English (the yearly bilan issued in May is particularly useful).

USEFUL INTERNET SITES

- **Ecran noir** http://www.Ecran noir.com
  A very comprehensive site unfortunately mostly in French.
- **France diplomatie** http://www.France diplomatie.fr
  Historical summaries and film fact files in English.
- **CNC** http://www.cnc.fr
  Comprehensive official database of the French film industry.
- **Unifrance** http://www.Unifrance.org
  Site devoted to the promotion of French cinema in the world. Contains articles and entries on many films.
- **Lumiere Centre**
  http://lumiere.obs.coe.int/web/FR/search.php
  Film database in English and in French.
- **BIFI** http://www.bifi.fr
  Site of the film library in Paris (includes archive and online catalogue).
- **Films de France** http://frenchfilms.topcities.com
  A useful database on French cinema available in English, including a section on the best of the New Wave.
- **http://iihm.imag.fr/truffaut/**
  A site devoted to the films of François Truffaut.

East Asian New Wave Cinema

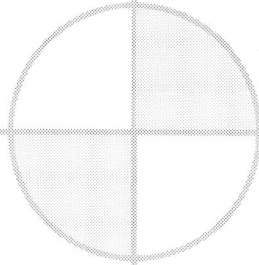

Introduction

East Asian cinema has offered one of the greatest challenges and alternatives to Hollywood. The combined cinemas of the region have made a huge impact all over the world from the Japanese masters such as Kurosawa to the martial arts of Bruce Lee, Jackie Chan and Jet Li. These and others have also influenced Hollywood directly - from crossover talent such as John Woo and Chow Yun-Fat to Hollywood's current trend of buying up remake rights to South Korean hits. This section of Alternatives to Hollywood explores the most innovative and ingenious leaders of this region, in short, the New Wave.

First it's necessary to attempt a geographical definition of East Asia. It's essentially what was once the Far East – a term post-colonial studies has deemed inappropriate. (Where is the East far from?) The countries can be listed as follows: People's Republic of China (including Special Administrative Regions Hong Kong and Macau), Japan, Democratic People's Republic of Korea (commonly known as North Korea), Republic of Korea (commonly known as South Korea) and Taiwan (also know as the Republic of China to confuse things!). Commonly the term excludes South or South East Asia (Indian Subcontinent, Vietnam, Thailand, Malaysia, the Philippines, etc.) and Central Asia. Some of these countries, especially Thailand and the Philippines, have a close cinematic relationship to East Asia and have the potential to be included but will not be covered here. For our purposes East Asia is Japan, China, Taiwan and Korea. Hong Kong, although now a Special Administrative Region (SAR) of the People's Republic of China, is still counted as a separate market by the film industry.

The first section, A Brief History of East Asian Cinema, offers an overview of all these cinemas recognising their similarities and differences while providing an historical context to their industries. Three movements are then singled out for specific attention – Hong Kong's New Wave (including an extended case study of director Wong Kar-wai), China's Sixth Generation and South Korea's latest New Wave. The next section then focuses on two case studies: *Suzhou River* (China 2000) and *Take Care of My Cat* (South Korea 2001). The final section offers recommendations for films, books and other resources.

Take Care of My Cat (South Korea 2001)

© Soda Films

What is New Wave cinema?

New Wave cinema has become a popular term in Film Studies as a way of grouping together a series of films and personnel that represent a change of direction or a break with the past. It is not a theory and neither is its meaning particularly stable. A New Wave is usually a historical moment within a national cinema. The most famous example is the French New Wave; essentially a group of young critics turned film-makers who broke with the previous traditions they called 'cinéma du papa' and made exciting, experimental and innovative films. Other famous New Waves include the British New Wave (more commonly called Free Cinema or Kitchen Sink), Polish and Czech New Wave and even New Hollywood where directors in the 1970s made groundbreaking films that reinvigorated the industry and broke old boundaries.

The traits of each New Wave will be different, but there are some common elements in East Asia:

- **Personnel** - The film-makers of the East Asian New Wave are nearly all educated abroad and they demonstrate an understanding of several cinematic trends, chiefly those of Hollywood, Europe and East Asia itself.

- **Economics** – The New Waves appear in prosperous climates with the finances to risk.
- **History** – Most New Wave films are set in the contemporary period but they still reflect the history and politics of the recent past. For example, Wong Kar-wai's films are never overtly political but are obsessed with times and dates which draw parallels with the handing back of Hong Kong to China. Where they are historically set they also appear to address current issues, for example, Tsui Hark's *Once Upon a Time in China* (1991) comments as much upon contemporary cultural imperialism as it does nineteenth-century colonialism.
- **Style** – The Hong Kong New Wave has led the way in visual style, especially in action and cinematography. For example, stylised violence in recent South Korean films is indebted to John Woo (see *Shiri*, 1999) whereas any film with a pretension for art will recall Chris Doyle's signature cinematography (indeed he works all over the region).

Increasingly the industries of East Asia are intertwined and interdependent, many actors work across several countries (Hong Kong's Cecilla Cheung in South Korean film *Failan*, 2001; Japanese-Taiwanese actor Takashi Kanashiro in Hong Kong's *Chungking Express*, 1994, and China's *House of Flying Daggers*, 2004). The opening up of the mainland Chinese market has also increased the number of co-productions and potential exhibition outlets, though piracy remains a huge problem. Films are not restricted to Asian co-productions either; they are often partly financed through other countries such as Germany or France (*Suzhou River*, *Balzac and the Little Chinese Seamstress*, 2003) or the US (*Crouching Tiger, Hidden Dragon*, 2000).

All film titles are referred to by their English titles, original titles may be accessed through the databases listed in the resources section. The names of people are written in the Eastern tradition with family names first, and I have adopted the most commonly used spellings in all cases (i.e. those found in industry magazines and press). Readers may come across articles with slight differences where a more formal translation approach is used.

A Brief History of East Asian Cinema

All of cinematic history is related, and cinema has crossed real and imagined borders since its inception. In fact during its early silent years it was by nature universally understandable and therefore travelled much easier. Cinema was invented, almost simultaneously, in the US, Britain and France and because of this has often been characterised as a foreign import in many places around the world. Yet only the technology was foreign; as the stories and experiences connected with audiences around the world.

Cinema has always therefore been the ideal instrument to explore the tensions between modernism and tradition. Whether in rural or urban areas, the issue of modernity and the conflict that follows it has been explored by many East Asian films. Cinema itself has a problematic relationship with modernism, for it is both strikingly obvious that it is artifice yet it represents reality clearer than any other art form.

Japan

Cinema arrived in Japan in 1897, brought by Inabata Katsutaro, who was a student in France with French cinema pioneer Auguste Lumière. Initially the main obstacle to cinema's development in Japan was the slow spread of electricity. Despite this, it quickly became extremely fashionable and was integrated into popular entertainment alongside theatrical traditions. All silent films were narrated by a *benshi*, who would stand by the screen to tell the story.

The industry was well structured from the start and directors were set up as the control stations; the notion of an *auteur* was in place long before the 'Cahiers du cinéma' critics claimed to invent it. This is why Japanese cinema history is often recounted through its directors, most famously Mizoguchi, Ozu and Kurosawa. Kenji Mizoguchi was famous for his melodrama and the *jidaigeki* genre (period drama), for example, **Ugetsu** (1954). Yasujiro Ozu was less well known in the West, and mostly explored contemporary life through the *gendaigeki* genre (contemporary drama) in films such as **Tokyo Story** (1953). Kurosawa achieved iconic status in the West (ironically he was less respected at home) for action films such as **The Seven Samurai** (1954). These three directors essentially made the 1950s the golden age of Japanese cinema.

The Japanese New Wave is a term given to a series of films and their directors in the late 60s. Nagashi Oshima is often heralded as leader of this unofficial group producing films such as *The Cruel Story of Youth* (1960). He later became infamous in the West for his arty sex film *In the Realm of the Senses* (1976) and then the popular Second World War drama *Merry Christmas, Mr. Lawrence* (1983) starring David Bowie. Other noted New Wave directors were Seijun Suzuki (*Tokyo Drifter*, 1966), Susumu Hani, Shohei Imamura and Masahiro Shinoda.

In the contemporary period, Japanese cinema is popular worldwide and films are made in virtually every genre imaginable. It would be unfair to reduce Japanese cinema to its three most visible outlets: animation (especially that from Studio Ghibli like *Spirited Away*, 2002), gangster (notably Takeshi Kitano films like *Violent Cop*, 1989) and horror (whether psychological studies like *Ringu*, 1998, or gory horrors from eccentric director Takashi Miike such as *Audition*, 1999). Even the directors most associated with those genres venture into other territories; Kitano with the serene *A Scene by the Sea* (1992) or *Dolls* (2002), or Takashi Miike's quirky musical *The Happiness of the Katakuris* (2001, interestingly a remake of an earlier Korean film *The Quiet Family*, 1998). Contemporary Japanese cinema has a high profile on the art house and festival scene with films like *Afterlife* (1998) and *All About Lily Chou-Chou* (2001) and crossover titles *Battle Royale* (2000) and *Zatoichi* (2003).

Given the focus here on 'New Wave' film, we have not considered particular case studies from Japanese cinema; but the influence of Japan over East Asia as a whole (whether historical, economical, cultural or cinematic) should not be underestimated. The effects of Japanese imperialism are reflected through films from the entire region, many directly about military conflicts, for example, *Hong Kong 1941* (Hong Kong, 1984) and *A City of Sadness* (Taiwan, 1989). All of the countries discussed below have a post-colonial relationship with Japan; the periods of Japanese intervention were Korea (1910 to 1945), Taiwan (1895 to 1945), China (1932 to 1945) and Hong Kong (1941 to 1945). More recently Japanese culture and style is extremely trendy and influential, from Hello Kitty and Pokémon to its unique cuisine through to ideas of minimalism in home furnishing.

The WJEC A2 Film Studies syllabus at the time of writing offers an option 'Japanese Cinema: 1950-1970' where students can study films from the golden age to the New Wave.

China

As in Japan, the first recorded film screenings were not long after those in the West, in 1896 at the Xu Tea Gardens in Shanghai. The Chinese referred to the films as *yingxi* or shadowplays, and also as 'Western peep shows'. The first film shows in Beijing, however, were not until much later (1902); yet it was here that the first film production began. Opening in 1905, the Fengtai Photoshop produced mostly Beijing Opera scenes in the style of foreign newsreels. When Fengtai Photoshop moved to Shanghai in 1909, it signalled the beginning of Shanghai as the country's film capital, which it remained for over 70 years. Throughout this period of early cinematic history, many Chinese entrepreneurs were quick to exploit the financial potential, and an uneven industry developed a trend of boom and bust.

For the period 1896 to 1949 in Chinese cinema history, it is important to stress the dominance of foreign film imports (and indeed personnel): over 90% of the films were from Hollywood. Furthermore, audiences were largely urban-educated in east coast treaty ports and film exhibition did not make significant inroads into the mainly peasant countryside until well after 1949.

The Shanghai industry of the late 1920s and 1930s is often referred to as one of Chinese cinema's 'golden ages', particularly because of the success of the *wuxia pian* (swordplay genre). The industry was never a fully fledged studio system but there were two 'major' studios: Mingxing Film Company (formed 1922) and Lianhua (1930), and three 'minor' studios: Yihua (1932), Diantang (1934) and Xinhua (1935). The studios were a battleground between the forces of the left (Communist sympathisers) and the right (Nationalist), with the Film Group set up by the left wing to promote Communist sympathisers in the industry.

The Japanese invasion of China that started in Manchuria in 1932 reached Shanghai in 1937 causing all the studios except right wing Xinhua to cease production. Some important films were produced during the war, notably **The Spring River Flows East** (1947-8), a three-hour epic (a kind of **Gone with the Wind**, 1939) following a husband and wife's separation through 1931 to 1945. The legacy of the 1930s industry is evident in all of the succeeding Chinese cinemas: personnel fled to Hong Kong and Taiwan and set up studios, while some remained and became key players in the post-1949 industry.

Zheng Junli's **Crows and Sparrows** (1949) was started before, but finished after, the civil war (1946 to 1949). This transitional period film focuses on the residents of an apartment block, literally the crows (right wing decadents) and the sparrows (honest, hard-working peasants). The Communist Party were already aware of the potential propaganda power of cinema; in the years after the revolution they nationalised the industry and phased out all foreign films except those from the Soviet bloc. They also sought to expand exhibition through mobile units and to make films that would appeal to the rural masses. Film-makers were forced to adopt Soviet social realism as their model, and the industry became dependent upon Soviet training and equipment.

Like the situation in Eastern Europe, Mao's regime had periods of 'thaw' (less restrictive government, e.g. during the Hundred Flowers movement) where quality production increased, and periods of 'freeze' (heavily restricted, e.g. during the Great Leap Forward) where production could not meet the targets and expectations. Chinese films of the 1950s and 1960s, such as Xie Jin's *Two Stage Sisters* (1966), display high production values and a polished look that belie their political agenda. Also in this period, the government opened regional studios and a national archive, while severing their links with the Soviet Union thus losing equipment and expertise. The first signs of the effect of the Cultural Revolution (1966 to 1976) on film were the extended official criticisms of certain films from mid-1964, including *Two Stage Sisters*. Fiction film-making was stopped altogether between 1966 and 1970, and after that only the limited production of 'revolutionary model operas' was permitted.

The film industry began to recover in the years after Mao's death (1976), following the introduction of reforms by the new leader Deng Xiaoping. The Beijing Film Academy reopened in 1978, and what became known as the Fifth Generation of Chinese film-makers enrolled. Sheila Cornelius (2000: 34) describes the new era of film-making as 'the two main legacies of film history in China – the human-realist tradition of the 1940s, and the socialist-realist tradition of the Cultural Revolution – combined with a new atmosphere of liberalism'.

Western scholarship of Chinese cinema has primarily been interested in this Fifth Generation, through a cannon of films and directors who have brought international acclaim to contemporary Chinese cinema. The most well-known directors are Chen Kaige (*Yellow Earth*, 1984), Zhang Yimou (*Red Sorghum*, 1987) and Tian Zhuangzhuang (*The Blue Kite*, 1993). Again, similar to the film industry in Eastern Europe, state support was withdrawn and film studios were forced to find private funds.

The Sixth Generation of film-makers reflect a new era in China's modern history, appearing to work with increasing freedom, though censorship is unpredictable at best. The generations do overlap; Fourth Generation director Xie Jin made the epic *The Opium Wars* in 1997, and all of the above-mentioned Fifth Generation directors have released films in the recent years (notably Zhang Yimou's *Hero*, 2002, and *House of Flying Daggers*). Leading Sixth Generation directors include Zhang Yuan (*Beijing Bastards*, 1993), Wang Xiaoshai (*Frozen*, 1997, *Beijing Bicycle*, 2002) and Lou Ye (*Suzhou River*). This generation has built up a reputation for headstrong independence, and their films often reflect the poverty and marginalisation of China's cities while demonstrating an international cinematic influence.

Hong Kong

Hong Kong has a rich cinematic history, starting in the first decade of the twentieth century, and a reputation for the concentrated production of popular films. The 1980s became the golden age of Hong Kong cinema, a vibrant and commercial industry that exported its local films over the Asia-Pacific region and to Chinese Diasporas all over the world. Through Bruce Lee, martial arts and University campus film theatres, America, duly followed by Europe, began to discover this exciting, eclectic cinema from the last remaining 'jewel' of the British Empire. However, the Hong Kong film industry has a history that long precedes its 'discovery' by the West.

The first film was made in Hong Kong in 1909 (*Stealing the Roasted Duck*) and by the 1920s the colony had emerged as a key centre for Cantonese dialect film-making. Until the 1970s this market was almost exclusively export-orientated for Cantonese speakers in China and throughout the Asia Pacific. The conflicts in mainland China brought about a relocation of the Shanghai film industry to Hong Kong in the 1930s and 1940s, producing a dominant Mandarin dialect cinema until the 1970s. The version of Cantonese spoken in Hong Kong is an indigenous dialect of the Pearl River Delta area around Guangzhou, and can be seen to represent a political stand or an agent of subversion against the official Mandarin dialect of the People's Republic of China (both are written the same). It has therefore been instrumental in the formation of a unique Hong Kong identity, both for the territory and the cinema industry alike.

In the 1950s the high rate of productivity and low quality established the idea of Cantonese movies being like fast food –

inexpensive, mass-produced, easily consumed and just as simply discarded. Cantonese movies died out, however, through the late 1960s and early 1970s primarily because of the popularity of Cantonese TV and the better quality Mandarin films. The martial arts genre brought Hong Kong cinema worldwide recognition in the 1970s. This was, however, something of a mixed blessing as it overshadowed all other genres in Hong Kong film-making, especially the melodramas and social problem films.

The Cantonese dialect films of the New Wave of the late 1970s and early 1980s marked a change of direction for the industry, one that brought Mandarin production to a virtual end. The New Wave was born out of post-war generational changes. Many of the film-makers had studied abroad and then returned to develop their talent in television. New directors such as Ann Hui planted Hong Kong on the international festival circuit, while the cult cinema of John Woo and Tsui Hark brought about the integration of the Hong Kong aesthetic with Hollywood. Following the belated Hollywood success of Jackie Chan in the 1990s, many of Hong Kong's finest talents – including John Woo, Chow Yun-Fat, Jet Li and Michelle Yeoh – departed there permanently.

The Hong Kong industry does not match the traditional model of a national cinema; instead it is greatly influenced by the Hollywood production model. Its exports, like Hollywood, have virtually destroyed the domestic production of many of its regional neighbours, most notably Taiwan. The small ex-colony has even achieved periods where its production exceeded that of Hollywood, impressive considering that, unlike most national cinemas, it has not received government funding until very recently. Hong Kong would go on to impact on all of East Asia's pop culture; it has become a capital in the region because of its strategic location, liberal society and its importance as a manufacturing and financial centre. As a result its films often display a transnational feel, shaped by their funding through pre-sales to its overseas market that includes Thailand, the Philippines and Japan. They retain a unique identity, foremost through their differentiation to the tradition of film-making developed on the mainland – namely the social-realist films of China's Fifth Generation directors.

The film industry, however, has been in decline since 1992, with a number of factors targeted as to blame: key personnel emigrating, triad involvement and extensive piracy (VCD copies are readily available on markets on the same day a new film opens). Despite this there have been some notable local hits and international successes like Stephen Chow's *Shaolin Soccer* (2000), Wong Kar-wai's *In the Mood for Love* (2000) and Andrew Lau's *Infernal Affairs* (2002).

Taiwan

Taiwan's film industry was established much later than in China and Hong Kong, starting with the Taiwan Motion Picture Association set up by the Japanese during the Second World War (the Japanese ruled the island between 1895 and 1945). This combined with the Taipei News Picture Association to become the Taiwan Film Studio, the industry developing out of and retaining features from its newsreel/documentary history. Several film-makers also fled to Taiwan with the retreating Nationalist (Guomindang) government in 1949, bringing elements of the Shanghai industry with them.

Through the 1950s, 60s and 70s government-owned studios produced much of the output, as much as 200 films annually. For example, in 1966, Taiwan was the third largest film-producing nation in Asia behind Japan and India. The industry, however, suffered greatly in the 1980s for a number of reasons, one of which was the flow of cheap Hong Kong imports. Despite the industry's problems a number of prominent directors have emerged under the label 'Taiwanese New Cinema' who have either moved to Hollywood (Ang Lee) or continue to produce acclaimed art house features (Edward Yang, Hou Hsiao-hsien and Tsai Ming Liang). International successes have been few and far between recently, the most prominent being, Edward Yang's *A One and a Two* (also known as *Yiyi*, 1999).

Korea

The history of film in Korea started in 1903 with the first public screening of a non-Korean film. It took at least another 16 years for the first Korean produced film to appear; the date and the actual film are still hotly debated by academics and critics, some claiming the first film appeared as late as 1923. The Korean film industry did not establish itself before the Japanese formally annexed the peninsula in 1910, subsequently enforcing its own monopolies and strict censorship. Korean produced films such as *Arirang* (1925) were, however, extremely popular and often contained discreet political subtexts for the native audiences. The Japanese, fearing this, restricted Korean productions to period or melodramas and pro-Japanese films until banning Korean language films completely in 1942. The majority of these early films were lost forever during the civil war (1950 to 1953).

In 1945, at the end of the Second World War, the Japanese surrendered and Korea was divided in two along the 38th parallel; the division to produce North (or the Democratic People's Republic of Korea) and South Korea (or the Republic of Korea). From here on, Korean cinema history, indeed the whole of modern Korean history, is also divided into two. Our attention is on the South, but by necessity rather than choice. North Korea has a significant film industry but unfortunately it is not accessible. As a generalisation following the division, North Korean cinema became a propaganda tool on the model of the USSR (and by extension Eastern Europe and mainland China) while the South became a capitalist industry like the US, Western Europe and Japan. Technically the two sides are still at war, a factor exploited in both cinemas (South Korea's **Shiri** is a good example).

In North Korea, Kim Jong Il – son of former dictator Kim Il Sung and now himself leader of North Korea – was appointed Director of Film Art in 1968. He wrote a book, The Theory of Cinematic Art, that has been the official guide for the film industry ever since. Kim, whose entire family is unrivalled in its control of the country, even famously abducted South Korea's leading director and his actress wife in 1978 forcing them to work in the North Korean industry for eight years. The state has total control over film and watching films is a compulsory activity, more likely to be found in a factory than a cinema. Films are mostly propaganda, though some are designed primarily for entertainment; either way they must adhere to the principles of 'anti-classism' and 'anti-Japanese nationalism' (the latter because North Korea refuses to acknowledge South Korea as a separate state, and instead blames foreign powers for the 'temporary' division). Reports from those who have left North Korea suggest that viewers may well see through the propaganda or find alternative readings for scenes that supposedly condemn opulence and affluence (perhaps even veiled references to the current rulers?), though evidence is scant. If we do ever gain sufficient access, there must be some excellent classroom case studies to be devised around what is essentially a country's cinema divided by political not cultural concerns.

Back in South Korea, the period of US occupation (1945 to 1948) has only five films in existence to define it, the rest destroyed along with most of the film-making equipment during the civil war. Following the cease-fire in 1953, foreign aid programmes enabled South Korea to rebuild the film-making infrastructure, and recovery was also aided by the government declaring cinema exempt from all taxes. The latter part of the 1950s and the majority of the 1960s are considered by many critics to be a golden age for South Korean cinema. Production increased dramatically, admissions surged and directors such as the extraordinarily prolific Im Kwon-taek (at the time of writing, ninety-nine films and counting) started their careers. The Motion Picture Law of 1962 stated that production companies must produce at least 15 films a year and their orientation should be commercial (at the expense of art or experimentation). Melodramas were extremely popular especially those of Kim Ki-young, a director rediscovered by academics in the 1990s, notably his *The Housemaid* (1960). On a similar theme was *The Houseguest and My Mother* (1961) by another popular director – Shin Sang-ok – this being the director abducted by Kim Jong Il as mentioned earlier (who then ended up working in Hollywood!).

The golden age did not last, the industry declined in the 1970s. This decline was often attributed to the popularity of TV, but was also a consequence of the turbulent social period and very strict government censorship. The decade ended at a low point with the tragedy of the Kwangju massacre in 1980 where around 200 pro-democracy demonstrators were killed by government troops. The industry recovered through the 1980s as new socially conscious talent emerged in a 'mini' New Wave. Two important factors were the relaxation of censorship and the lifting of import restrictions, meaning both greater freedoms but greater competition. Park Kwang-su's *Chilsu and Mansu* (1988) marked the first political film to be released after the relaxed censorship. Film critic Tony Rayns ('Sight and Sound', November 1994: 22) discusses the relevance of politics for the young Korean directors, and its difference to the Chinese Cultural Revolution's impact on the Fifth Generation:

> The equivalent primal trauma for the young Koreans was the uprising and massacre in Kwangju in May 1980, the shocking event that sparked off 13 years of ferocious anti-government activism and (in 1993) led to the end of militarist rule and the election of South Korea's first civilian president, the former oppositionist Kim Young-Sam. The Koreans, in other words, were marked by an event more like the 1989 Tiananmen Square massacre than the protracted collective mania of the Cultural Revolution.

The significance of the Kwangju massacre cannot be underestimated and, though unique to Korea, the influence of political history on cinema is discernible throughout East Asian Cinema from oblique references to the hand-over in Hong Kong New Wave films to the trauma of decades of colonialism and suppression in Taiwan.

Hong Kong New Wave

The first Hong Kong New Wave was born out of post-war generational changes. Many of the film-makers had studied abroad and then returned to develop their talent in television. The New Wave was representative of a new age and became an internationally renowned cinema. Unlike others elsewhere, however, this New Wave was still subject to the commercialism and conventions of Hong Kong popular cinema. Hong Kong popular cinema at its commercial best is exemplified by the comedy martial arts of Jackie Chan and the action-violence of John Woo.

The first New Wave of Hong Kong cinema arrived in 1979 with aspirations to make a cinema of social significance and stylistic breakthrough. The 1970s was a time of socio-economic transition in Hong Kong, with problems of increased manufacturing through cheap labour, housing shortages, drugs, prostitution, police corruption and organised crime.

The dominance of the Kung Fu genre also laid the groundwork for the emergence of the Hong Kong New Wave. As the French New Wave before them, the Hong Kong one was in part a reaction against the 'cinéma du papa' as the French had called it. Despite the fact the group was not a cohesive group, they all shared an attempt to produce a new style for a new generation that was bored by their generic legacy. The New Wave was characterised by subject matter dealing with youth: school, sex, drugs and other traits of growing up in a materialistic society, misunderstood by parents and authority. The films had a more relaxed structure and rhythm, and often a direct, quasi-documentary style. The camera was more mobile and the performances more naturalistic. The New Wave was a comprehensive group including writers, designers and cinematographers. The New Wave also tried to break with the tradition of poor scriptwriting that did – and still does – plague Hong Kong cinema.

Although the New Wave produced a record number of young *auteurs*, Hong Kong was still a commercial dream factory that depended on a star system, and unabashedly stuck to the principals of mass entertainment. Although the New Wave brought better quality control, its directors adhered for the most part to the same principals of commercial entertainment. The best films of the first New Wave come towards the end: *A Chinese Ghost Story* (1986), *A Better Tomorrow* (1986), *Rouge* (1987) and *Song of the Exile* (1990).

By the mid-1980s the first New Wave had integrated with the mainstream industry, or a few became well-established *auteurs* such as Ann Hui (*Song of the Exile*). At the same time a 'second New Wave' appeared, not collectively as the first, but with a definite continuation of the aims of the first. Film-makers of the second New Wave include Wong Kar-wai and Fruit Chan (*Made in Hong Kong*, 1997). Mostly trained in overseas film schools, this group of directors were largely the assistants of the first wave. The mid-1980s directors also began to address the question of Hong Kong's return to Chinese rule in 1997, known as the 'China syndrome'.

The 'China syndrome' developed from the early 1980s negotiations about Hong Kong's future, and explored the relationship between China and Hong Kong. The idea of kinship and cultural affinity was marred by undertones of political anxiety and fear, especially after the events of Tiananmen Square in 1989. Questions of identity, nationality and ethnicity permeated Hong Kong cinema, but manifested themselves more complexly in the New Wave cinema. Hong Kong cinema, and Hong Kong itself, has always meant engaging with the two differing, and often oppositional, (film) histories of the West and the East/China. This concept will be explored in the case study of Wong Kar-wai below.

Director Case Study: Wong Kar-wai

Wong Kar-wai emerged under the banner of the New Wave in 1988 with the commercial hit, *As Tears Go By*. An immigrant from Shanghai at the age of five, he worked (with no formal training) as a scriptwriter for several years, most notably on Patrick Tam's *Final Victory* (1986). As a director, Wong Kar-wai is something of an anomaly to the Hong Kong film industry. In a fiercely commercial trade he has consistently found funding, produced 'artistic' films and attracted the top stars despite poor domestic returns. He has been helped by his films' success on the international festival and art house circuit, creating a reputation as a world innovator in his field. This has also, however, dislocated him from his Hong Kong context in terms of the film industry, location and cultural space, which are all very prominent themes in his films.

Wong Kar-wai, although often scriptwriter, director and producer, is not the 'grand *auteur*' but rather the 'band leader' of his creative team, including long-term collaborators Christopher Doyle (cinematographer) and William Chang (artistic director and editor). Both Wong and Chang are immigrants from the mainland, and the Australian born, self-trained Doyle has worked in the Hong Kong and Chinese film industry consistently after establishing his reputation with Taiwanese director Edward Yang's *That Day, On the Beach* in 1983.

As Tears Go By, Wong Kar-wai's directorial debut, is an important place to start for several reasons. Firstly, it locates Wong firmly within Hong Kong cinema, a context he has become detached from in his later films as his visibility on the international art house circuit increased. Secondly, it was a commercial success locally and especially in Taiwan, starring popular local actors. This enabled him to find finance for his next and very different project, *Days of Being Wild* (1991), and also signalled the start of his working relationship with some of the biggest stars in Hong Kong. Thirdly, and most interesting, it is Wong's most overlooked film, the proverbial black sheep of his film canon, for reasons discussed below. This third reason is linked to the first; the film lies so uncomfortably with his others because of its sense of local and its generic heritage of the Hong Kong action movie. Yet it still displays some of the stylistic traits and innovation of Wong's later films.

Wong Kar-wai would have been unlikely to start his career with a film like *Days of Being Wild* because of commercial pressure, but *As Tears Go By* should not be rejected or criticised for its market success. Wong's later films were still financed commercially but this time by foreign investors from countries such as Taiwan. None of Wong's later films were to reach the popular success of *As Tears Go By* in Hong Kong; all received a luke-warm reception at the home box-office.

As Tears Go By is Wong's most commercial film (both in terms of box-office success and accessibility), and his closest to the Hong Kong mainstream in terms of genre and narrative. The film follows the story of the middle-rank triad Ah Wah (Andy Lau), his unpredictable 'little brother' Fly (Jackie Cheung), and his promising relationship with his cousin, Ah Ngor (Maggie Cheung). Ah Ngor comes to stay with Ah Wah because she has to visit a nearby lung specialist. At the time she visits, Fly is causing trouble with another local triad gang who brutally beat up Fly and his little brother. Ah Wah avenges Fly, starting a series of revenge attacks that ultimately lead to their downfall. In an effort to recover his dignity, Fly accepts a job to kill a police informant in custody. Fly shoots the informant but is then shot himself; Ah Wah avenges Fly's death and is also shot dead. Ah Wah and Ah Ngor's relationship develops through the film, from early sexual tension in his flat to a caring relationship when he visits her on Lantau. She plans to move to Kowloon and live with him before the tragic ending.

The film's themes of brotherly kinship and warring triad factions display the influence of the Hong Kong gangster-hero genre especially John Woo's *A Better Tomorrow* (1986), and touches of American influences such as *Mean Streets* (1973). Hong Kong cinema has a tradition of borrowing from Hollywood, one that has recently become a reciprocal arrangement, albeit to the detriment of the industry. Wong's influences would later expand to European cinema, but *As Tears Go By* is so firmly within the Hong Kong style that the audience at the Cannes Film Festival, unfamiliar with the genre, found it shockingly violent.

A Hong Kong film audience is accustomed to expecting a sequel to popular films, but they were never to receive one from *As Tears Go By*. Though the star presence was magnified, *Days of Being Wild* bears little resemblance to its precursor. Wong Kar-wai's subsequent films were never to match his debut's popularity at home; but as his films became less popular at home they became more popular abroad.

Days of Being Wild revolves around Yuddy (Leslie Cheung) fostered by a rich Shanghainese woman who denies him the identity of his real mother. Yuddy, an arrogant playboy, seduces Su Lizhen (Maggie Cheung), only to end their relationship when she wants commitment. He then dates the showgirl/dancer Mimi (Carina Lau) on whom his poor best friend Zeb (Jackie Cheung) develops a crush. The rejected Su takes to stalking Yuddy's neighbourhood at night, consoled by the stoic policeman Tide (Andy Lau). Tide invites Su to phone him at a public phone box on his beat, but by the time she does he has changed career and gone to sea.

Yuddy's foster mother, Rebecca, about to emigrate to the US, is pushed into revealing the location of Yuddy's affluent mother in the Philippines. He immediately departs for there, leaving Mimi heartbroken and Zeb his car. After a failed attempt to woo Mimi, Zeb sells the car to buy her an air ticket for Manila. Yuddy's real mother refuses to see him and Yuddy ends up drunk and mugged in Chinatown. He is rescued by Tide, who is waiting for his ship to sail. Tide is forced into Yuddy's irrational confrontation with a Filipino gang over a fake US passport, the outcome of which is that Yuddy is shot attempting to escape on a train from Manila. The film ends with a strange coda introducing a new character (played by Tony Leung), preening himself for a night out on the town.

Days of Being Wild is a slow paced, poetic, opulently visualised trip to 1960s Hong Kong, a city of immigrants and loners with a quiet stillness presumably now lost forever. Like *As Tears Go By*, time passes indeterminately, but here it takes a more central role visualised through multiple clocks, watches and chance encounters. If time has a co-conspirator it is space; places and distance create the moods and loves of the characters, feelings only realised when they have gone.

The title credits of *Days of Being Wild* are accompanied by scenes of blue-tinted palm trees moving past – a brief flash-forward, out of context. When it is repeated near the end of the film, it reminds the viewer of the early scenes that surrounded it, the opening sequence with Yuddy and Su at the stadium where she works. This has the effect of a *déjà vu* of images for the audience and of memories for Yuddy. Memories are as unreliable as nostalgia; Yuddy and Tide cannot recall their first meeting, just as Hong Kong too has trouble with its past. Hong Kong has no pre-colonial history to speak of; since colonisation, it has grown into a central port for all of Asia, characterised by the transferral of goods and shaped by immigration, leaving no definitive cultural 'past'.

The Chinese title of *Days of Being Wild* literally translates as *Rebel Without a Cause*, and the character of Yuddy is immediately identified as this rebel – slick hair and clothes, a fast car and many girlfriends. Unlike the brotherhood and gangland camaraderie on display in *As Tears Go By*, Yuddy is an isolated and ambiguous character.

The appearance and clothes of Yuddy (sharp outfits, American car) reflect an era in which foreign influence increased dramatically. The characters (especially Yuddy and Rebecca – Shanghainese immigrants) use wealth and fashion as a method of separating themselves from the culture of the motherland. There is little trace of the traditional Confucianist family values at work in *Days of Being Wild*; instead the characters operate individually, free of ties. While there is a family unit, it is illegitimate and dysfunctional: Yuddy's foster mother is revealed to care only because of the money she received to do so. She also believes that her wealth is sufficient affection for Yuddy.

The experience of the characters is placed outside of mainland China; Su comes from Macau, a Portuguese colony further along the

Pearl River Delta. Macau has an even longer history of foreign influence than Hong Kong: colonised in the seventeenth century, it has also developed a cultural identity remote from the mainland. When the protagonists leave Hong Kong (as most do), they depart for the US, Philippines or just to drift on the open sea (as Tide does). Their eclectic destinations reflect their sense of rootlessness; Su feels no ties to Hong Kong or Macau and is therefore left isolated (literally pictured alone in the stadium where she works). It is not that Chinese culture is denied in Hong Kong, but it must be acknowledged as changed by the tensions created by its history and foreign influence.

The un-named agent (played by Brigette Lin) in **Chunking Express**

© BFI Stills

Chungking Express is a film of two halves, two stories about unlucky in love policemen navigating through a distinctly urban Hong Kong. In the first story, Cop 223 (Takeshi Kaneshiro) has been dumped by his girlfriend May on April Fool's Day. He counts down the days up to his 'deadline' for her to return (1 May 1994 – also his birthday) by every day buying a tin of pineapples that have an expiry date of the 1 May 1994. At the same time, a drug dealer's agent (Brigitte Lin) is preparing a group of Indians in Chungking Mansions to smuggle drugs by air. The Indians escape from her at the airport and the agent seeks revenge by shooting them and later her western drug dealer boss. Cop 223 realises May is not coming back and eats all the pineapple. He then goes to a bar, throws up and promises himself that he will fall in love with the next woman who enters the bar. The agent arrives and they end up spending the night in a hotel, but she only sleeps while he eats. The next day he goes running, and is overjoyed when the agent bleeps him a happy birthday.

In the second story, Cop 663 (Tony Leung) buys a chef salad every night from the Midnight Express takeaway for his girlfriend. When the owner suggests he takes her a choice, she is prompted to change not only her diet but also her boyfriend. She leaves him a letter and his spare keys at the takeaway, where a young girl Faye (Faye Wong) dreams of flying to California. Faye begins to fall for Cop 663 and uses the keys to enter his flat when he is not there. She tidies, rummages and replaces objects within his flat until she is caught out. Cop 663 then asks her out, but she stands him up, instead going to California, though she leaves him a 'boarding pass' for a year later. When she returns, Cop 663 has bought the Midnight Express and asks her to draw him up a new pass, destination anywhere.

The opening sequence of **Chungking Express** introduces the location of Chungking Mansions, a large run-down mixture of stalls, curry houses and cheap hostels. As a central location for the first part of the film, it makes up half of the title, the later part referring to the Midnight Express location of the second half, a food takeaway. Chungking Mansions is significant because of its awkward placing within the tourist 'golden mile' of Tsimshashui, on mainland Kowloon. Inside, it is atypical of the surrounding area, a compressed, densely populated city centre of luxury hotels, shops and Chinese tourist restaurants. Chungking Mansions is also congested, but a paradoxical sense of isolation pervades through its Indian diasporic population and the many closed stalls with the metal shutters down. It has a not entirely undeserved reputation for crime, but is still accessible for backpackers and hungry tourists.

The technical style of the opening scenes are part of cinematographer Christopher Doyle's signature style (as he describes it): 'blurred action sequences with the adrenaline rush triggered by fear or violence' (Doyle, 1997, p.15). The hand-held camera follows both the agent and Cop 223 around Chungking Mansions: one is breaking the law, the other enforcing it. The camera pauses to linger on empty rooftops, blue sky and drifting clouds. The long shot moves to a ground level position looking up between the tall housing blocks. There are quiet, open spaces in the urban city, but these images remain outside of the characters' perspectives: perspectives that reside exclusively in the blurred conurbation below.

Chungking Mansions represents a theme of multiculturalism and globalisation in Wong Kar-wai's work. This is not straightforward, however, as the representation of Indians is problematic: they are presented as double-crossing drug smugglers ordered around like naughty children by the hard-faced agent. The western character fares no better, an unfaithful arrogant dealer, who makes it clear that the agent has an 'expiry date' (printed on the sardine tins he leaves for her) and forces his conquests to wear garish blonde wigs.

The global influence is through commodities (the Garfield cat, western music) and through the use of language. The Chinese protagonists often communicate in other languages; the agent speaks in English with the Indians and the Filipino bar girl; Cop 223 in Japanese, English and Mandarin as he attempts to chat the agent up. Before the hand-over Hong Kong was officially bilingual: English and Cantonese, though other dialects such as Shanghainese could and indeed still can be found there. In *Chungking Express* the local language and cultural signs are mixed freely with others, and the ease with which this is accomplished demonstrates the extent to which Hong Kong has formed (and been formed by) notions of multiculturalism.

Faye represents the laissez-faire capitalism at work in Hong Kong, as she works solely to buy frivolous commodities and to travel. The 1990s were a time when many people left Hong Kong or at least opened up a 'get out' clause (e.g. obtained a foreign passport) in case things took a turn for the worst in 1997. This also represents Hong Kong's transitory spirit, the result of its history of immigration and free-port status mentality. Even though Faye returns she is now professionally in transit – as an airhostess, always prepared to fly away again.

Times, dates and especially expiry dates are ever present in *Chungking Express*. In the first half the date of 1 May 1994 is all consuming; it is the date of Ho's (Cop 223) deadline and birthday, and also the date for the agent to complete the drug deal. This date is seen printed on Ho's cans of pineapple and the agent's sardine can; the days are counted down on an old-fashioned flip-over clock-calendar. The characters' voice-overs describe the future at the time they will occur; 'In 24 hours I will fall in love with this woman' and, 'In 6 hours this woman will have fallen in love with someone else'. Ho later laments, 'Is there anything that doesn't have an expiry date?' It is compelling to regard the obsession with times and dates in terms of Hong Kong's own obsession with its 'expiry date' of 1 July 1997. The characters want to escape their expiry dates, put them back (Ho wants an expiry date of 10,000 years for his birthday message) or leave to avoid them (the agent and Faye fly off). Interestingly, only the agent appears to depart permanently; Faye returns and the rest are likely to stay, a subtle form of optimism for the future incorporated into the film.

Chungking Express was shot over a few weeks break from Wong's rarely shown martial arts epic, *Ashes of Time* (1994) – actually an excellent slow burning, star-studded art house film, the precursor to Zhang Yimou's *Hero*. Wong Kar-wai's next film *Fallen Angels* (1995) is the natural sequel to *Chungking Express*, especially in style and narrative, and therefore is his least original film. This is also a sort of ultimate postmodern gesture, using a playful self-referentialism – Chungking Mansions, Midnight Express, pineapples, flat re-arranging and airhostesses all reappear in *Fallen Angels*.

The story again intertwines two tales of unlucky in love city-dwellers, this time concurrently with no division. Wong (Leon Lai) is the hit man who works with his agent (Michelle Reis) remotely. The agent (unnamed throughout) organises both his professional and domestic life, arranging hits and cleaning his flat. Back in Chungking Mansions, an ex-con mute, called He (Takeshi Kaneshiro), lives with his father, raiding other people's businesses after hours and coercing some into paying him to leave them alone. The killer, Wong, decides to end his partnership and also embarks on a casual relationship with the eccentric Baby (Karen Mok).

Whilst pursuing his nocturnal activities, He meets and falls for the recently jilted Charlie, and helps her to plan revenge on her ex's new bride-to-be, the allusive 'Blondie'. He later realises that she is unlikely to return his affection, so he instigates change by taking on a job at a Japanese restaurant. The owner, a former film director, produces home videos of himself for his family back in Japan, giving He the idea of recording his father's daily activities. Wong decides to terminate both his relationships with 'partners', but agrees to one last fatal assignment. He's father dies and the home videos become a poignant memory for He. The film ends with He meeting up with the agent in a bar brawl and giving her a lift home on his motorbike.

The film employs some unusual stylistic traits to create a darker, neo-noir world than *Chungking Express*, this time shot exclusively at night. Wide-angle lens are used to distort the environment and characters, effectively creating distance in small spaces and suggesting a separation between them despite their physical proximity. Doyle describes the effect: 'our notionally taboo wide-angle lenses are being brought in more and more often, to make a "flat" image more "interesting"'('Sight and Sound', May 1997: 16). Time is also distorted through editing. Larry Gross observes:

In Fallen Angels *he shows the killer's agent preceding him through a scene of an assassination, but later he intercuts their movement to condense and smash the logical temporal sequence together, so the editing process illustrates their proximity, their desire and the impossibility of its fulfilment.* ('Sight & Sound' September 1996:9)

The time and space of **Fallen Angels** perpetuate the recurring themes of isolation and rootlessness as the postmodern urban affliction. Would-be couples in both films appear in long still scenes together, where the world spins fuzzily around them. This relatively low-tech sequence is produced by the actors moving very slowly against the 'normal speed' world around them. For Charlie and He, their scene is in black and white; they are together physically but the technique reveals their real isolation. It also exaggerates the 'mean streets' of Hong Kong, where if you are not shot by an assassin you could be force fed ice cream by a persuasive mute.

In reality, Hong Kong is not a dangerous city; it has low crime rates and a prominent police force. The return to the generic base of **As Tears Go By** means that **Fallen Angels** actually has more in common with the typical violent Hong Kong cinema of its time (such as **Young and Dangerous**, 1995 and **Once Upon a Time in Triad Society**, 1996) than a global art house audience might expect. These generic features (gangsters, crime, stars and comedy) reinforce the film's relationship with Hong Kong and its popular culture. The effect of Wong Kar-wai films on the independent local market cannot be underestimated either, as films such as **Fallen Angels** have clearly influenced the work of Fruit Chan and others, provoking Wong Kar-wai to claim, 'too many other directors are doing a Wong Kar-wai these days, so I have to do something different'.

Happy Together (1997) opens with the familiar motif of travel and time: two passports are opened and stamped 12 May 1995. This film can be regarded as following the Wong Kar-wai characters from previous films (such as Rebecca in **Days of Being Wild**, the agent and Faye in **Chungking Express**) that left Hong Kong but whose stories were not told. It is ironically significant that their departure and arrival somewhere else is signified by another expiry date stamp. Their passports are clearly marked 'British National Overseas' – an ambiguous identity (inasmuch as it does not provide right of abode in the UK) – which also has an expiry date, the deadline of 1 July 1997. Even though the protagonists are no longer in Hong Kong, they cannot escape its future and the consequences of its socio-political situation.

The film is about the turbulent relationship of Ho (Leslie Cheung) and Lai (Tony Leung), and their attempt to 'start over' in Argentina. They initially intend to visit the Iguaza Falls by car, but end up lost and separated. They arrive independently in Buenos Aires, where Lai takes a job as a doorman at a tango club and Ho becomes a hustler. Their relationship is rekindled when Ho arrives at Lai's small flat, badly beaten, Lai taking up the job of nursing him back to health. As Ho gets better their relationship once again deteriorates; Lai hides Ho's passport in an attempt to prevent him leaving. Ho starts to see other men, and Lai makes friends with Chang (played by Taiwanese actor Chang Chen) in a Chinese restaurant where he is now working.

Chang and Lai's platonic friendship develops, and with Ho virtually out of the picture, Lai plots his journey home. Before Chang departs on his own travels, Lai tells him about a lighthouse 'at the end of the world' where one can dispose of one's problems. Chang asks Lai to privately relate his problems into a tape recorder, and Lai is unaware that Chang later 'releases' these at the lighthouse. Lai supplements his income hustling and works at an abattoir, eventually returning home to Hong Kong via the Iguaza Falls and Taipei (capital of Taiwan). Lai calls into Chang's family restaurant but he is not there, and Ho visits Lai's empty apartment and retrieves his passport.

Happy Together is unique in Wong Kar-wai's canon because of its depiction of a homosexual, rather than heterosexual, relationship. This is typical of Wong Kar-wai's mature work in its rootlessness and blurring the norms of conventional narrative and genre. *Happy Together* is a sort of gay road movie-melodrama. It is refreshingly open in its representation of the gay relationship, and though it deals with the issue of prostitution it steers clear of the stereotypical cinematic themes of AIDS and homophobia. The story of two gay men can be placed in a context of the international New Queer Cinema movement, as well as a product of Hong Kong cinema.

The film was a minor revolution for Hong Kong cinema in that it foregrounds the identity of non-heterosexual characters. Hong Kong cinema has no fixed history of dealing with homosexuality (except a few comic interpretations) so it came as a shock to the local audience to see two of its major stars, Leslie Cheung and Tony Leung, embrace with frank intimacy. The actors are extremely physical in their roles, both in constant movement throughout, reflecting the turbulent chaos of their relationship. There are two scenes of real intimacy – in the back of a taxi and when they tango together. Here the film literally slows down (using the 12 frames per second technique Wong employed in his earlier films); the moments feel stretched in comparison to the rest of the film. During the taxi scene the film also erupts into colour, emphasising the sense of real intimacy. Later Ho reminisces about their embrace via a flashback while dancing with another man, but, typically of Wong Kar-wai, time has left Ho behind, and Lai has since departed for Hong Kong.

In addition to those discussed above, Wong Kar-wai has directed three more films to date: *Ashes of Time, In the Mood for Love* and *2046* (2004), all of which can also be analysed using the methods above. Wong Kar-wai himself discusses the relevance of *2046*:

> The idea of the film came in 1997. In those days just before the hand-over, the Chinese government promised 50 years without change. In the film there is a place called 2046, because after 50 years there will be no places, only numbers. It will be a utopia. There in 2046 they think nothing will change. The film is set in the future, but it's more about now. I want to talk about people trying to preserve something that they have inside, but they are afraid what they have will be lost. It's nostalgia happening in the future. ('Newsweek International', 21 May 2001:60)

The films of Wong Kar-wai articulate a cultural space for Hong Kong throughout its transitory period (1984 to 1997). Through their distinctive use of time and space, Wong's films represent an urban experience unique to a society faced with the prospect of its own disappearance (integration with China). The first film, *As Tears Go By* in 1988 reflects the period after the future of the colony had been confirmed but before the alarming events of Tiananmen Square in 1989. In 1991, *Days of Being Wild* responded to a wave of nostalgia for a 1960s colonial past that revealed the colony's 1990s crisis of legitimacy. In the mid-1990s, *Chungking Express* and *Fallen Angels* depicted a postmodern Hong Kong, integrated within a global culture, conscious of its hybrid identity. In the early part of the hand-over year itself, *Happy Together* offers an optimistic solution in its ending, a reconciliation with China (and even perhaps China with Taiwan) that may open up new possibilities for both cinema and society.

China's Sixth Generation

Cinema history in China has been defined by generations of its film-makers. This grouping together of films and directors does help to chart the development of the film industry and the types of film it has produced, though it should not be approached as prescriptive as there are many exceptions and anomalies. The previous generations are roughly: the early pioneers; the directors of the 1920s (mostly martial arts films); the 'golden age' of the 1930s and 1940s; the Soviet inspired cinema of the 1960s, followed by the Fifth Generation of the 1980s. The generations also loosely match the graduating classes of the Beijing Film Academy, which was closed (like other universities) during the Cultural Revolution.

The Sixth Generation are the mainland Chinese directors who emerged in the 1990s, often defined as the post-Tiananmen Square 'urban generation'. They break with many of the traditions of the Fifth Generation, the most noticeable shift being a concentration on the urban present rather than a rural past. Richard Corliss, writing for 'Time Asia', describes the change from Fifth to Sixth Generation as, 'a night at the Peking Opera gives way to an all-nighter in the Beijing mosh pit'. The concentration is on ordinary people in their urban mundane lives. Though the Fifth Generation used ordinary people, they instead set them against the huge backdrop of China's modern history.

The film industry has also changed dramatically. The studios must now be responsible for their own profits and, although there are restrictions, there is no longer a state production, distribution and exhibition monopoly. Many of the Sixth Generation films were made outside of the state studio system, as independent underground productions, sometimes illegally. Wang Xiaoshuai made his first film, *Frozen* (1996), under the pseudonym of Wu Ming (literally 'no name') to avoid persecution. *Platform* (2000) was saved from its funding problems by Japanese *auteur* Takashi Kitano. Censorship is an ongoing concern; famous incidents include Zhang Yuan getting his passport revoked over *East Palace, West Palace* (1996), and several films have been taken out of China to be edited.

The Sixth Generation had a different social, political and cultural experience to those before them; they were mostly too young to be directly involved in the Cultural Revolution. Tiananmen Square was a defining moment for them, especially as most were students at the time. They also appeared to share a dislike of the Fifth Generation films, of their subject matter and style, and the fact that they seemed to have 'sold out'. There are also directors like Dai Sijie, who have left China, but returned to film his autobiographical tale *Balzac and the Little Chinese Seamstress* (based on his novel of the same name).

The experiences of the Sixth Generation directors are also of the period following Deng Xiaoping's economic reforms and the opening up China to the west and capitalism. This created unequal wealth distribution with old people, low wage earners and academics particularly suffering. This period is also characterised by heavy migration from the rural to the urban, and an influx of western brands such as McDonalds. The government, however, retained tight control of the press; ironically the foreign press who reported on Tiananmen Square where actually there to cover Russian leader Mikhail Gorbachev's visit to China. Especially critical of the problems created by the economic reforms is director Jia Zhang Ke, whose films (including *Platform*, 2000) criticise the contradictions of a society caught between two opposing value systems.

Not a unified movement, the Sixth Generation share several themes and styles. Nearly all are about disillusioned youth in major conurbations, with themes of sex, drugs, crime, poverty, commercialism, pop culture and striving for identity. The predominant style is documentary influenced – a neo-realist aesthetic (e.g. hand-held cameras, non-professional actors), that stands as a sharp contrast to the well crafted, colourful films of the Fifth Generation. Again, in contrast to the earlier films, the individual is now prized over the communal or epic, arguably a post-Cultural Revolution, post-Tiananmen suspicion of collectivism. Despite this, there are also plenty of exceptions and variety in the films, for example, Jia Zhang Ke's *Platform* is a period film covering 1979 to 1989 that bears the influence of Taiwanese director Hou Hsiao-Hsen and European art cinema film-makers such as Robert Bresson. Lou Ye's *Suzhou River*, however, owes more to the *Chungking Express* school of MTV aesthetics and editing, while also being indebted to Alfred Hitchcock's *Vertigo* (1958).

Case Study: *Suzhou River* (Lou Ye, 2000)

Sixth Generation director Lou Ye made his name through Chinese TV and pop videos, before breaking through with his second feature film, **Suzhou River**. A story of love lost, found and lost again, **Suzhou River** fulfils many of the requirements of the Sixth Generation (urban location, ordinary people) while having a sense of magical realism (visually upbeat, strange coincidences and unconventional romance) absent from virtually all other Sixth Generation films.

The story is essentially that of two pairs of lovers: the unseen narrator and Meimei (a showgirl who dresses as a mermaid for her act in a seedy bar); and Mardar (a motorcycle courier with gangland connections) and Moudan (the teenage daughter of one of Mardar's clients). Mardar and Moudan gradually fall for each other, and spend their days on his motorcycle drinking her father's illegally produced buffalo vodka. Mardar is then forced by his gangland connections into an unsuccessful kidnap of Moudan for a ransom. On finding out her value in money to Mardar, Moudan jumps off a bridge into the river. Her body is not found.

Many years later, Mardar enters a bar to find a girl in a blonde wig and mermaid costume, Meimei – she is not only the double of Moudan but dressed exactly like the mermaid doll Mardar gave to Moudan as a present. Mardar is convinced she is his

Moudan, and his path crosses with Meimei's boyfriend (the unseen narrator) who is threatened by the obsessed Mardar. The narrator arranges for Mardar to be beaten up and he leaves. The narrator receives a note from Mardar saying he has now found Moudan working in a shop. Later the bodies of Mardar and Moudan are found in the river, and the four are finally brought together. Meimei realises Mardar was telling the truth about Moudan and she runs away, leaving a note for the narrator.

The complex narrative builds up layers it never quite resolves, but this is the intention, to create a sense of *déjà vu* through an unreliable and indeterminate narration. Much of the film is shot with a hand-held subjective camera, the camera is literally what the narrator sees and we do not see the narrator. In one scene he hands over the camera's point of view to Mardar, the shot fades to black briefly as he literally closes his eyes on the story. There is also a blurring of the boundary between his eye and the camera, as he is a videographer. Sometimes he is using a camera and then occasionally we glimpse a body part that means the point of view is not his eye or his camera.

The narrative also rests heavily on the strength of the lead actors, and they both deliver strong, detailed performances. Jia Hongshen (Mardar) brings the appropriate roughness to his character (often attributed to his experiences as a former drug addict) and is also known for his portrayal of the suicidal performance artist in *Frozen* (1996). Zhou Xun (Meimei/Moudan), a popular TV actress, started her career with a small role in Chen Kaige's blockbuster *The Emperor and the Assassin* (1999) before taking the dual leads in *Suzhou River*. Since this film, Zhou has gone on to appear in several internationally acclaimed hits (that can also be described as New Wave) from China and Hong Kong including *Beijing Bicycle*, Fruit Chan's *Hollywood, Hong Kong* (2001), *Balzac and the Little Chinese Seamstress* and *Baober in Love* (2004).

The visual style of the film makes playful reference to a range of influences – mostly obviously the films of Wong Kar-wai, French New Wave, Hollywood film noir and Hitchcock. From Wong Kar-wai and the French New Wave, Lou Ye borrows jump cuts and a quirky hand-held camera; from noir and Hitchcock some scenes display a rich, dark tension and often frame Meimei/Moudan as the innocent/dangerous femme fatale.

The parallels to Hitchcock's *Vertigo* are obvious – a man believes an almost identical woman to be his former dead lover and despite his efforts to change the second love story she also ends up dead. Enhancing the reference is German composer Jorg Lemberg's soundtrack, purposefully echoing Bernard Hermann's *Vertigo* score. Yet *Suzhou River* is far from a remake or even reinterpretation, with the narrative departing swiftly from the initial *Vertigo* premise. The gender politics are also more complex; Mardar tries to make Meimei into Moudan, yet Meimei is just as obsessed, attempting to make the narrator into Mardar. Meimei is distraught to discover Mardar really did think she was Moudan, and was not simply inventing a story to romance her. She challenges the narrator to go to the lengths that Mardar went to for Moudan, and disappears leaving only a note for him that says, 'find me if you love me'.

The film also reflects issues of globalisation for China and the influence of the west on China's society. The mermaid motif is from a western myth that has never appeared in Chinese traditions, therefore symbolising outside influence on the city and its stories. *Suzhou River* is an international co-production, with funding predominately German, then Chinese, French, Japanese and Dutch. There were no censorship issues during production as it was shot with a TV production licence which is not as strict as a film one. The film, however, has still not been commercially released in mainland Chinese cinemas at the time of writing.

Director Lou Ye, a native of Shanghai, attended the Beijing Film Academy with many other directors of the Sixth Generation. His graduation film, *Weekend Lover* (1994) is an early example of the issues and themes of the Sixth Generation. The film follows a group of disillusioned youth in urban Shanghai, a counter attack to the Fifth Generation's obsession with tradition and history. Lou Ye then produced an influential and experimental television series, *Super City* (1995), on which several other young Sixth Generation directors also worked. He founded one of the first independent production companies, Dream Factory in 1998. Perhaps a sign that the Sixth Generation is widening its remit, Lou Ye's third film, *Purple Butterfly* (2003), is a period drama about anti-Japanese underground fighters in 1930s Shanghai and stars Zhang Ziyi (*Crouching Tiger, Hidden Dragon*, *Hero*, *The House of Flying Daggers*).

Extract analysis: Closing sequence (DVD chapters 11 and 12)

The narrator and subsequently Meimei have discovered the bodies of Mardar and Moudan. Meimei is in shock after finding the story Mardar told to be untrue, and that he was in love with her not Moudan. She is close-up talking to the camera, to the narrator that we have never seen. All that is really known about the narrator is that he is a videographer and he constantly films the world around him. Therefore, it is unclear here (as it many other parts of the film) whether he is actually filming Meimei or if the subjective camera is a substitute for his eyes.

'If I left you would you look for me? Like Mardar?' says Meimei. These are the words that opened the film against a black screen, and the conversation is repeated but this time it is clearly Meimei talking. Unlike the opening conversation this one carries on; 'things like that only happen in love stories.'

As they continue the conversation, the narrator's hands appear reassuringly caressing Meimei's head. This makes the camera the narrator rather than the narrator simply holding the camera. There is a dissolve cut to virtually the same scene, which instead of expressing a passage of time (as it frequently does) actually gives the impression of the narrator's strength of affection for Meimei. The voice-over reinforces this as he says he feels like they're back in old times. He then reminisces, saying how he sat up all night watching videos he had shot of her. There is a cut back to these earlier scenes as she moves playfully and seductively before the narrator's camera (now a hand-held camera rather than his eyes). She actively meets the camera's gaze then closes her eyes as he strokes her hair again, recalling the earlier scene.

The film cuts to the narrator (identified still by the voice-over) walking to Meimei's houseboat. This style is intentionally clumsy, the hand-held camera reinforces the documentary aesthetic; the narrator claims to be a documentary, rather than fiction, film-maker. Meimei has left a note saying, 'find me if you love me'. The next shot subverts the documentary aesthetic, however, as the camera literally becomes the narrator's face as he is pouring the vodka into his mouth (just below the camera). His legs are strewn out on the boat below, his body is slumped and his feet pointing towards each other, suggesting he is already drunk. There is the sound of the vodka being gulped down his throat. His voice-over adds, 'It was the best damn drink I ever had', a line straight out of a film noir.

As he sails down the river the voice-over continues. He contemplates chasing after Meimei or going back to his flat to look out from the window, but he decides not to 'because nothing lasts forever'. The music is especially important here, the Hitchcock inspired eerie beats getting louder as if to question the narrator. Suddenly the camera (therefore the narrator) falls to one side, to hang drunkenly and awkwardly over the edge of the boat. 'So I'll just take another drink and close my eyes...' The screen blacks out, '...waiting for the next story to start'. Was the whole story merely in the mind of this drunken man that we never see or never really know?

South Korean New Wave

The South Korean New Wave (or 'latest New Wave' as it is also called) emerged around the mid-1990s and was evident across other forms of popular culture such as music. Young people (and, of course, film directors) were exposed to the international media unlike any previous generations, and found that they had a new freedom and stability to explore their culture and society. Many of the directors of this New Wave were schooled abroad and their work shows influences of contemporary and historical cinemas from across the globe. This is one of many comparisons that can be made with the Hong Kong New Wave; another is the sheer range of films produced from action to art house.

As described above, the turbulent century of modern Korean history started with Japan's involvement in the early 1990s. Before that, the Choson Dynasty had reigned with relative calm for over 500 years, and Korean culture and language were distinct from its closest neighbours, China and Japan. After the division and civil war, US-supported South Korea took over 40 years to reach a fully functioning democracy with military regimes and social unrest frequent features. At the end of the 1970s, military leader Park Ching-hee was assassinated, though his replacement (General Chun Doo-hwan) proved equally strict. In 1980, a clash between government troops and pro-democracy student demonstrators resulted in 200 dead. This was to become known as the Kwangju massacre, predating a similar clash that garnered more media attention internationally – the Tiananmen Square massacre in China in 1989.

A gradual shift to democratic reform took place throughout the 1980s, and the early 1990s saw a renewed optimism. South Korea became one of the success stories of the pan-Asian economy (one of the 'four dragons'). Large companies such as Samsung invested heavily in the film industry at this time and equipment was upgraded, providing the industry with the tools, if not quite yet the inspiration, to operate on the world stage. The Asian financial crisis of 1997, ironically, was the final jolt for the industry; the large companies pulled out leaving small companies and innovative fundraising techniques (such as Internet shares known as netizens) that allowed further experimentation and creativity. As Anthony Leong condenses:

> Thus it was in the 1990s that the final pieces of the puzzle fell into place, jump starting the latest 'Korean New Wave': relaxed government censorship, investments in infrastructure, entrepreneurial zeal, and an iconoclastic attitude. (2004:10)

The domestic films have consistently built up their market share since 1997 with admissions on the whole increasing as multiplex building strives to meet demand. Up to date figures for the Korean film industry, including the box-office share for domestic films, can be found on the Korean Film Council's website (see Resources). The real success story of South Korean cinema is in its international sales figures: a growth of 60% from 1999 to 2000, and a further 56% the year after. Asia has been its most receptive audience (especially Hong Kong and Japan), with France, the US and finally the UK picking up more titles for distribution (and, in the US case, for remakes). International festivals have also boosted South Korea's profile, for example, high profile awards at Cannes (Tarantino personally endorsed Park Chan-wook's **Old Boy** during his stint as Jury President in 2004). Korea also has its own increasingly successful Pusan International Film Festival, taking the baton from previously popular festivals Golden Horse, Taiwan and the Hong Kong International Film Festival.

The first notable films of the New Wave were popular hits such as **Christmas in August** (1997) and **The Contact** (1997). **Shiri** introduced the notion of a Korean blockbuster, a film that could compete in a market saturated by high concept Hollywood. The film follows three special agents, one of them turning out to be a female undercover North Korean spy who lives in South Korea. 'Shiri' is actually the name of a fish that is only found in a lake in the demilitarised zone between the two Koreas, underpinning the message of peace and reunification stressed by the football match between the two states. The film contains set action pieces inspired by Jerry Bruckheimer's and John Woo's films, notably the latter's use of slow music over action. Another film that explores the North-South relationship is *Joint Security Area* (2000) which beat the box-office record previously set by *Shiri*.

Korean cinema is no stranger to one of the staple genres of East Asia – the gangster film. *Friend* (2001) is one of the most accomplished offerings, following four friends' stories over 20 years, all connected to the criminal underworld. The film was successful in appealing to a wide demographic: older audiences enjoyed the historical background, while younger audiences were wooed by the stars and MTV visual style. *My Wife is a Gangster* (2001) and *My Sassy Girl* (2001) are hit comedies that have gained a reputation in the west as sparking bidding wars in the US for remake rights. *My Wife is a Gangster* is a hilarious, if sometimes violent, film about a female gang boss who looks for a husband to please her dying sister. It is important to note that there is no direct relationship between New Wave and art house, even though there are films that can be described as art house in the New Wave.

South Korea's censorship is now in the form of the Media Ratings Board set up in 1995, less powerful than the previous government board, operating in virtually the same way as Britain's British Board of Film Classification (BBFC). There are further comparisons with the BBFC: their classifications are General, 12, 15, 18 and an uncommon Restricted. Sex and homosexuality are the biggest taboos, with Wong Kar-wai's *Happy Together* refused a certificate for a year until cuts were forced. As in many other countries, most film-makers are forced to make any necessary changes and follow the system due to commercial pressure.

Case Study: *Take Care of My Cat* (Jeong Jae-eun, 2001)

Take Care of My Cat is the feature film directorial debut of Jeong Jae-eun, who being a woman is very much in the minority in the Korean film industry and the latest New Wave. The story revolves around a group of five friends and their passage into independence and adulthood after graduating from high school (they are around 19 years old). Hae-joo is the most affluent and spoilt of the group, having pulled strings to get what first appears be a good job in a broker's firm. The others even joke about her 'princess syndrome', mostly ignoring her incredibly selfish ways. Ji-young is the most offended by her, a talented textile designer who can't afford to continue her studies, and lives in a shanty house with her grandparents, as her parents are dead. Tae-hee lives with her comfortable middle class family and she works at her father's business for free. She is the peacekeeper and catalyst for the group, constantly bringing them together as they drift apart. The final two of the five are half-Chinese twins, Bi-ryu and Ohn-jo who aren't really the focus of the film though they offer comic relief in their outings around Chinatown where they sell home-made fashion accessories.

The narrative switches between the five characters and is punctuated by their infrequent gatherings - a birthday, a day out in Seoul and a sleepover party. The title refers to Titi (subtitled in some versions as Tee-tee), the stray cat found by Ji-young that ends up passed between the five friends. The lost cat is a kind of metaphor for the girls struggling with their independence and their lack of direction. It can also be interpreted as a superstitious omen, as the girls' lives seem to change after looking after the cat. The film represents one of the more sophisticated and stylish of the Korean New Wave, foregrounding female experiences in an empathetic yet not stereotypical fashion.

The visual style of cinematographer Choi Yeong-hwan is often simple and unobtrusive, sometimes hand-held with the occasional quirky feature, especially the use of text messaging. In the opening scenes we see Hae-joo text a message to Tae-hee; the phone display appears on the right hand side of frame (recognisable by the universal signal and battery strength symbols, though the text is in Korean so appears as standard subtitles in English). A similar technique is utilised while Tae-hee types up poems for a disabled writer; the words she types appear across the table on which the typewriter is sat. A deep focus shot evokes Wong Kar-wai's style (especially in *Fallen Angels*); an office block dominates the left of the frame while a busy neon-lit street sits on the right. Unlike anything seen in a

Tae-hee (Bae Doo-na) in **Take Care of My Cat**

Wong Kar-wai film, however, the text message from Hae-joo to Tae-hee scrolls up the wall of the office block that divides the screen. What is said in text messages is ultimately significant too, here Hae-joo says, 'Sorry I can't go with you. Have a good visit. Say hi to Ji-young for me. Hae-joo'. Hae-joo makes it sound like Tae-hee is meeting Ji-young for a drink rather than visiting her in a young offender's institute. All of Hae-joo's communications reveal her selfish interests, her barely concealed self-importance and her arrogance. The film is very much about communication and the apparent fallibility of modern interaction by text and telephone. Messages can be misunderstood and are no substitute for personal interaction. Ji-young even stops talking altogether, following her tragedy, only to be brought round by Tae-hee's visits and positive actions.

The use of the landscape is original and another trait of the New Wave: the girls live in Inchon, an unglamourous industrial town about 25 miles from Seoul. It visually and narratively stifles their existence; huge cranes, a heavy fishing industry, homeless people and unsafe housing are all around them. This is a feature common to many New Waves: a poor urban setting, rather than glamourous, often period, locations.

Take Care of My Cat is hard to define generically; there are influences from teen films, docu-drama and social realism. It is driven by its well-rounded characters rather than a dramatic narrative structure, and in this respect it has more in common with a European art house film than Hollywood. The acting is excellent; Bae Doo-na (Tae-hee) in particular has received several awards for her part, and is a rising star in Korea.

The independence of the lead characters is emphasised through the absence of parental authority figures. For the twins and Ji-young only their grandparents are seen and Hae-joo's parents are barely glimpsed leaving the divorce courts. Hae-joo also has to waive away her last family tie, her sister, leaving only her put-upon would-be suitor Chang-young. Tae-hee's are the only parents that are seen, but her father is a patriarchal stereotype (encouraged by her brother), bossing her and the family around while her mother stays mute. The family situation forces her to symbolically cut herself out of the cheesy family portrait that hangs above the mantelpiece.

Extract Analysis – Opening sequence

Note: At Press time (summer 2005) **Take Care of My Cat** *was unavailable on R2 DVD, hence the absence of frame stills to illustrate this analysis.*

Take Care of My Cat opens like a conventional coming of age film, the girls are celebrating their graduation – screaming, dancing and taking photos – seemingly inseparable. Immediately the next scene is a sharp contrast that establishes the tone for much of the film: while the opening is sunny and the port looks attractive in the background, suddenly the skies are grey, a couple are heard arguing and a window is smashed. We see Hae-joo set off for work, and later events explain the window as we find out her parents are getting divorced. The tension at home explains her desire to get a job (instead of going to university) and become independent. She walks past a car with its windscreen smashed out, either a result of her parents' conflict or a symbol of urban decay. The title reveals the area to be 'East Inchon Station' with the many roads, railways panning out over the port signalling an industrial city.

After reading and staring out of the window, Hae-joo sends a text message: 'You're probably still sleeping. See you tomorrow at Club 369 at 7:00'. The message appears as a mobile phone screen superimposed onto the right of the frame, a unique visual feature. The text sounds innocent, though with hindsight we realise she is texting Tae-hee about her birthday, and her reference to 'still sleeping' is more likely a dig at Tae-hee working for her father and the fact she doesn't have a long commute to Seoul (and by implication to a real job). Hae-joo is glimpsed opening the blinds of her office with a glass wall in the foreground decorated with a basic map of the world made up of black squares. The squares are the graphic match to Ji-young's later textile drawings, a subtle comparison of their status and careers. Opening the window to the sounds of the street below, Hae-joo then straightens a desk that appears to be hers before her boss surprises her with an early entrance, and one of her patronising speeches.

The film cuts to Tae-hee typing, sat in a bedroom with a young man in bed and the light that falls though the window in a manner that suggests stuffiness. The mise-en-scène is composed of right angles and straight lines – the bed, desk, window and a bar across the bed – all create a feeling of restriction. The young man, it is revealed later, is a poet who suffers from cerebral palsy and Tae-hee gives up her spare time to help him. The words that she types appear along the desk underneath her typewriter, allowing the viewer to read the poem and hear Tae-hee's comments on it. The old fashioned typewriter rather than computer emphasises the notion of modern technology separating rather than connecting; the poet claims her coming to type for him is the only way he can see her.

The twins are introduced in the next scene; immediately they are comic relief, struggling to carry a large DHL package to their grandparents. They switch carrying positions, but it is still impossible to tell them apart (even their close friends confuse them later in the film). They only communicate with their grandfather through the one-way video monitor at the door, their faces appearing in wide-angle on a small blue monitor for their grandfather to see. Again modern technology is separating rather than connecting people. The twins' scenes nearly always contains flashes of red – shop fronts, signs in Chinese, and later as one of their Cheongsam dresses that Hae-joo tries on. The same red is echoed in Tae-hee's gloves; could it stand for luck as it does in Chinese culture? Bright red is also the colour of Ji-young's prison outfit so perhaps it is not so lucky, although the fact she is in the juvenile delinquent centre gives Tae-woo the impetus to find a way to change their lives.

The last of the five to appear is Ji-young (played by former fashion model Ok Ji-young) who walks dejectedly down a derelict street. A voice-over relates what is presumably an earlier conversation between her and her former boss, the latter asking her if she had a new job and explaining she would be paid when the equipment was sold, implying the business is in difficulties. She finds a stray cat and takes it home despite her Grandmother's warnings that, 'cats are supernatural, you shouldn't keep them at home'. Ji-young reprimands her for her superstitions, but ironically tragedy later strikes the house. The camera cuts to Ji-young playing with the cat on her bed, the unusual camera angle and composition meaning that her grandparents are visible through a window that diagonally dissects the upper right hand of the screen. This reveals the close, cramped conditions of the shanty house they live in, practically on top of each other.

The introductory scenes are completed by showing Tae-woo again, but this time in her domestic context. She arrives home to clearly a large affluent house but one distastefully decorated. She is affectionate to her younger sibling but straight away her father is on her case. He berates her non-stop about the time she has arrived home, her volunteer work, her not eating. He even shouts about her room being locked ('no wonder it's all mouldy'). Her room is an escape from her father, and her mother barely seems to feature in her life at all. In fact none of the girls' mothers are influential (no others are even shown on screen), a comment on the changing role of women in contemporary Korean society and perhaps the mothers' inability and inexperience to help their daughters with this.

Sample Questions
(Elements of answers in italics.)

- Discuss the chief characteristics of East Asian New Wave cinema, with specific reference to two films of your choice.

  *This answer should explore the areas of personnel (film-makers, stars), economics, history, style as outlined in 'What is New Wave cinema?' above. Students are encourage to then choose two films from one country (for example, **Take Care of My Cat** and **My Sassy Girl** from South Korea) or two films that share similar concerns from different countries (for example, **Suzhou River** from China and **Chungking Express** from Hong Kong).*

- Analyse the relationship between East Asian New Wave cinema and contemporary Hollywood including a consideration of financial motivation in the film industries of both regions.

  This question is aimed at students understanding and comparing the film industries rather than the cultural differences of the films. The answer could use examples of recent remakes of Hong Kong or Japanese films, and should also demonstrate how market concerns influence production, distribution and exhibitions of films.

- Discuss the importance of stardom in East Asian New Wave cinema with specific reference to one actor.
  Students can look at the concept of stardom, and those related to it such as performance and fandom, in relation to domestic stars from any cinema (for example, Zhou Xun in China, Bae Yong-joon or Han Suk-kyu in South Korea – the latter interestingly always compared to Tom Cruise) or international East Asian stars like Chow Yun-Fat or Zhang Ziyi.

- How are young people and youth culture represented in East Asian New Wave cinema?
  This answer can draw on examples from across the regions finding parallels and differences through themes such as relationships, family, urban life and the media. The visual style, music, influence of the west and urbanisation can also be considered.

- To what extent is the future of East Asian New Wave cinema in co-productions both regionally and internationally?
  This question specifically addresses the industry and students should have a range of examples of co-productions to draw upon. They should also consider how this influences the films made, for example, the co-productions necessitate using stars and locations from over the region.

- Discuss the involvement and representation of women in East Asian New Wave cinema.
  Students can discuss women as film-makers (for example, **Take Care of My Cat** *director Jeong Jae-eun, Hong Kong director Ann Hui) or stars such as Maggie Cheung and Zhang Ziyi.*

- How is the concept of *auteurism* relevant to East Asian New Wave directors?
  There are many case studies of directors to consider such as Wong Kar-wai, Fruit Chan, Kim Ki-duk, Jia Zhang Ke and Wang Xiaoshuai. Students should balance a consideration of auteurism with reference to the characteristics of New Wave cinema.

- How in your opinion does East Asian New Wave cinema offer an alternative to Hollywood?

This question is open and students can choose to discuss industry concerns or themes and styles of any East Asian New Wave film. Students, however, should decide a focus for their answer to avoid an answer that lacks depth or generalises too much.

Selected Filmography

• Hong Kong New Wave

A Better Tomorrow (Ying huang boon sik)
Dir. John Woo
Hong Kong 1986 Cantonese 95m
UK DVD available

John Woo is perhaps the best known Hong Kong director internationally with Hollywood blockbusters like **Face-Off** (1996) and **Mission Impossible II** (2000) to his name. For many critics, however, he has never surpassed his golden age in Hong Kong with genre-defining gangster films like **Hard Boiled** (1992) with Chow Yun-Fat. **A Better Tomorrow** demonstrated Woo's ability to combine New Wave aesthetics with hyper-real action sequences and spawned the Hong Kong trend of 'heroic bloodshed' films. The film's use of choreographing fight scenes in slow motion to a classical soundtrack has been copied in many films from B-movie action flicks to **The Matrix** (1999). The story centres on two triads, Mark (Chow Yun-fat) and Ho (Ti Lung), the latter whom goes straight for the sake of his younger brother, policeman Kit (Leslie Cheung). Unfortunately, Ho is double-crossed on his 'last job' and end ups in prison. Their father is killed because of Ho's connections, and Mark sets out to avenge the death with dramatic consequences.

A Chinese Ghost Story (Sinnui yauman)
Dir. Ching Siu-tung
Hong Kong 1987 Cantonese 98m
UK DVD available

Though directed by Ching Siu-tung (and fight choreographed by him) **A Chinese Ghost Story** is also heavily indebted to its more famous producer, Tsui Hark. Tsui Hark is also a director with an impressive filmography including **Peking Opera Blues** (1986), **Once Upon a Time in China** (1991) and **Twin Dragons** (1992, with Jackie Chan). Tsui was also at the forefront of the Hong Kong New Wave with **Butterfly Murders** (1979). **A Chinese Ghost Story** is a ground-breaking fantasy, a remake of **The Enchanting Shadow**

(1958) which was based on a novel by popular Ming Dynasty writer Pu Song-ling. Leslie Cheung (who committed suicide in 2003) plays a naïve tax inspector who falls in love with a beautiful ghost (played by Joey Wong) who happens to be held captive by an evil tree demon. The film is a perfect example of east-west hybridity combining western horror and MTV aesthetics with traditional Chinese spirituality and Hong Kong martial arts and comedy.

Chungking Express (*Chong qing sen lin*)
Dir. Wong Kar-wai
Hong Kong 1994 Cantonese 102m
UK DVD available
See above section on director Wong Kar-wai.

Comrades: Almost a Love Story (*Tian mi mi*)
Dir. Peter Chan
Hong Kong 1996 Cantonese 118m
US/HK DVD available
Peter Chan is a distinguished Hong Kong director and producer who has also worked in America. His films are popular yet intelligent, from comedies such as *He's a Woman, She's a Man* (1996) with Leslie Cheung to horror films such as *Three* ('Going Home' segment, 2000) and *The Eye* (2002, producer). *Comrades: Almost a Love Story* is a unique and sophisticated Hong Kong romance starring Maggie Cheung (after a two-year break from her career) and Cantopop star Leon Lai. Li Xiao-Jun arrives in Hong Kong from the mainland as an economic migrant who befriends local, clued up girl, Chiao. Chiao it turns out is also an immigrant but from nearby Guangzhou and Cantonese speaking. They go their separate ways, Li's fiancé comes to Hong Kong and Chiao marries a triad boss. However, their paths cross again at a contemplative moment in their lives. The film explores Chinese identity and nationalism in Hong Kong at the time of the hand-over to China.

Fallen Angels (*Duo luo tian shi*)
Dir. Wong Kar-wai
Hong Kong 1995 Cantonese 90m
UK DVD available
See above section on director Wong Kar-wai.

Made in Hong Kong (*Xianggang zhizao*)
Dir. Fruit Chan
Hong Kong 1997 Cantonese 108m
UK VHS available
Boldly marketed as the first independent Hong Kong film after the hand-over, ***Made in Hong Kong*** is a dramatic change to the majority of the industry's output. It was made in true low budget New Wave style with a cast of non-professional actors, a crew of five, set in unattractive cramped housing estates and shot on leftover pieces of film. This debut film from director Fruit Chan (now well established in the Hong Kong industry) was helped a little on its way, notably by executive producer Andy Lau, who is an extremely famous singer and movie star in Asia. The film is about disenchanted young people, especially Moon (played by Sam Lee, who the director spotted skateboarding on the street) and his mentally disabled friend Sylvester. Moon falls in love with a girl called Ping and attempts to help her and her mother escape the triad debt collectors the father had left them with. ***Made in Hong Kong*** explores the underbelly of the Hong Kong capitalist dream, a reminder that the surface glamour can be scratched to reveal an urban disgruntled youth stifled in their attempts at an identity.

Rouge (*Yin ji kau*)
Dir. Stanley Kwan
Hong Kong 1987 Cantonese 96m
UK VHS available
Stanley Kwan, like fellow *auteur* Ann Hui, has undeservedly never received the recognition garnered by other stand out directors such as Wong Kar-wai. Both make emotional, moving films that sit somewhere between art and commerce, and often concentrate on everyday Hong Kong characters. Despite ***Rouge*** being part-costume drama, part-ghost story it is also about contemporary Hong Kong society and identity. Executive produced by Jackie Chan, the story follows 1930s courtesan Fleur (Anita Mui, the actress known as the Madonna of the East) as a ghost in the 1980s, whom after committing suicide in a pact with her lover is now searching for him through a newspaper's missing person ads. The film also reflects the nostalgia evident in 1980s and 1990s Hong Kong, a sense of the colony searching for its roots before it is 'lost' to the mainland. The film sadly also takes on a renewed significance as both of its talented stars died in 2003; Leslie Cheung committed suicide while Anita Mui died of breast cancer.

Song of the Exile (*Ketu qiuhen*)
Dir. Ann Hui
Hong Kong/Taiwan 1990 Cantonese 100m
HK DVD available
A graduate of the London Film School, Ann Hui worked in television before launching her career as a film director with *The Secret* (1979), a hit thriller with actress Sylvia Chang in the lead. She garnered critical acclaim and Cannes screenings with her 'Vietnam trilogy' including *The Boat People* (1982), starring the now megastar Andy Lau. *Song of the Exile* is a fictional yet partially autobiographical story about a mother and daughter relationship and covers wider issues such as the impact of colonialism on identity. The film is set in the 1970s with some flashbacks to the young mother, juxtaposing the values of modern and traditional woman. The protagonist, Hueyin, grew up in Macau torn between her Chinese grandparents and Japanese mother. Hueyin has no real empathy or affection towards her mother, until she visits her mother's homeland and begins to realise what it feels like to be a foreigner.

• China's Sixth Generation
Beijing Bicycle (*Shiqi sui de dan che*)
Dir. Wang Xiaoshuai
China/Taiwan 2001 Mandarin 113m
UK DVD available
Beijing Bicycle contrasts two young 17-year-old males: one a stubborn migrant worker from the countryside (Guei) who is intent on earning enough to buy his bike from his employers, and a wealthier city student (Jian) who embodies a teenage preoccupation with commercialism, pop culture and status. Guei is about to own the bicycle when it is stolen, and in a nod to the inspirational source film – the Italian neo-realist classic *The Bicycle Thieves* (1948) – he cannot work without it. He is intent to get his bike back from Jian, who purchased it on the black market after stealing money from his father. Beijing is a bustling urban centre, switching between the locals of the shops and fast food restaurants and the hutongs, traditional tight residential alleys that make up roughly a third of the city. The film garnered critical acclaim through international festivals including a Silver Bear at Berlin in 2001. See *Frozen* below for information about the director Xiaoshuai.

Frozen (Jidu Hanleng)
Dir. Wang Xiaoshuai
China 1996 Mandarin 99m
US DVD available
Wang Xiaoshuai originally trained as a painter before enrolling at the
Beijing Film Academy. His first two films reflect his first career
choice, his debut *The Days* (1993) was about two artists and was
shot with his friends during free weekends. *Frozen* follows a young
avant-garde performance artist whose final act is his suicide. The film
is a rare glimpse of China's underground culture and explores the
alienation of youth in post-Tiananmen China. *Frozen* was illegally
shot (i.e. without government approval) and when released Wang
credited himself as 'Wu Ming', literally 'no name'. This was because he
had started work on his third feature, *So Close to Paradise* (1998)
that *was* government supported, though also about rural migrants
forging an existence in the city.

Platform (Zhantai)
Dir. Jia Zhang Ke
China/HK/Japan/France 2000 Mandarin 154m
UK DVD available
After the international festival success of *Xiao Wu* (see below)
director Jia Zhang Ke was able to get international funding for his
next ambitious film project, *Platform*. A major backer was the
production company of acclaimed Japanese director, Takashi Kitano.
The film follows a group of young performing artists through the
period 1979 to 1989 (roughly Chairman Mao's death to the time of
Tiananmen Square). The group becomes a mirror of cultural and
socio-political changes, literally going from communism (Mao songs)
to capitalism (western style rock music). The young people also live
in a remote part of China, represented in a distinctive visual style of
long takes and open spaces to create a mood of alienation and
dissatisfaction.

Shower (Xizao)
Dir Zhang Yang China 1999 Mandarin
UK DVD available
Director Zhang Yang started out in China's underground music
video scene and broke into features with his highly successful
independent film *Spicy Love Soup* in 1997. The producer of
Shower and *Spicy Love Soup*, Peter Loehr, set up Imar Film Co. Ltd,
the first legal independent studio in China, and one exclusively

dedicated to working with first time directors to make films for the urban youth. In **Shower**, a wealthy businessman, Er Ming, is forced to acknowledge his working class roots and reconnect with his father and brother who run a bathhouse. He goes from his affluent, modern life in Shenzhen (an industrial town in the special economic region near Hong Kong) to an ageing suburb of Beijing, where the bathhouse is facing demolition. The film juxtaposes new (modern) and old (traditional) China, via its interaction with family values and commercialism.

Suzhou River (*Su Zhou He*)
Dir. Lou Ye
China/Germany 2000 Mandarin 83m
UK DVD available
See above section on **Suzhou River**.

Unknown Pleasures (*Ren Xiao Yao*)
Dir. Jia Zhang Ke
China/Fr/Japan/SKorea 2002 Mandarin 113m
UK DVD available
Jia Zhang Ke's third film continues his exploration of China's underprivileged youth and their struggle against the system. The two main characters, Xiao Ji and Bin Bin, are unemployed teens whose journey culminates in their separation during an attempt to rob a bank. One chooses to flee discreetly while the other sings pop songs to the police. This ending seems to represent the dichotomy between quietly blending in and outwardly criticising with the implied reprisals this brings. Mass media as well as society is attacked by director Jia; the bored young boys are shown in a media saturated environment, their only socialisation is through video games, karaoke, television and films.

Xiao Wu
Dir. Jia Zhang Ke
China/HK 1997 Mandarin 105m
UK DVD available
Xiao Wu and his later film **Platform** were both set in director Jia Zhang Ke's native Fenyang County, Shanxi Province, and his films reflect his experience of growing up there. His family were not peasants but sent to the rural inland during the Cultural Revolution. Xiao Wu is the name of the main character, a pickpocket stranded on the margins of society. Jia uses a grey, bleak documentary

aesthetic style to emphasise his critique of the society. The film sympathises with Xiao Wu and condems the society that produced him and its hypercritical values. For example, his friend, a businessman, rebuffs him for his criminal ways yet he is shown to be corrupt (albeit in a way that benefits the system). Unsurprisingly, the Chinese authorities banned it at script stage but Jia found private investment to complete his film.

• South Korean New Wave

My Sassy Girl (*Yeopgijeogin geunyeo*)
Dir. Kwak Jae-young
South Korea 2001 Korean 123m
HK/Korean DVD available
Director Kwak Jae-young returned after a seven-year break from films with this box-office smash. *My Sassy Girl* is a comedy based on real life postings on the Internet. A naïve college student Kyun Woo (TV star Cha Tae-hyun) falls for a beautiful girl he finds drunk one evening. He vows to save her but it's not as easy as he thinks as her behaviour spirals out of control. *My Sassy Girl* is an unpredictable rom-com that plays with this and the teen drama genre. As with most South Korean hits, Hollywood (DreamWorks) has the US remake rights and British director Gurinder Chadha is currently attached.

My Wife is a Gangster (*Jopog manura*)
Dir. Cho Jin-gyu
South Korea 2001 Korean 107m
HK/Korean DVD available
This film gained a reputation when several US producers broke into a bidding war for the US remake, with Miramax being the eventual winner. Allegedly they had only seen an unsubtitled print, which suggests it will be the idea behind, rather than the essence of, the film, that will be remade. *My Wife is a Gangster* turns the Asian gangster genre around to focus on female mob boss Cha Eun-jin, who has unparalleled fighting skills. Her only weakness is her dying sister, whose last wishes are for Cha to find a husband. Cha attempts this the only way she knows how, to send her largely incompetent gang out to do it for her. The film's juxtaposition of comedy and violence is not unusual for the genre, but its subtle exploration of patriarchal society and femininity is.

Shiri (Swiri)
Dir. Kang Je-gyu
South Korea 1999 Korean 125m
UK DVD available
Shiri is often cited as the first Korean blockbuster (beating the previous box-office record held by **Titanic**, 1997) and is an interesting comparison to most Hollywood products, especially as it cost a fraction of the price. **Shiri** is an espionage thriller that centres on special agents Ryu and Lee, searching for an elusive North Korean assassin. The plot is complicated by tension between the special agents, Ryu's forthcoming engagement and an impending large-scale terrorist attack. Director Kang Je-gyu avoided the generic tendency to exaggerate or rely solely on special effects. As a result, the film competently explores the complex tensions created by a nation divided politically rather than culturally.

Spring, Summer, Autumn, Winter... and Spring (Bom yeoreum gaeul gyeoul geurigo bom)
Dir. Kim Ki-duk
South Korea/Germany 2003 Korean 103m
UK DVD available
Director Kim Ki-duk surprised critics with this gentle tale of an elderly monk and his young pupil set in a small monastery in the middle of a serenely beautiful lake. Kim's earlier works, although uncompromising and violent, are actually also slow burning 'art' films like this one. **Spring...** uses the seasons to reflect the pupil's stages in his life; each season is an episode in his life, in chronological order. The film is also part moral fable: the monk warns the young pupil who has tied some small animals to stones that if they die he will carry that stone in his heart forever. When the pupil returns in summer his hands are blood-soaked after killing his unfaithful wife in a fit of rage. The film is a visual mediation on the recurring cycle of life, each season defined by its colours and natural changes of the environment.

Sympathy for Mr Vengeance (Boksuneun naui geot)
Dir. Park Chan-wook
South Korea 2002 Korean 121m
UK DVD available
Sympathy for Mr Vengeance is the first in what director Park Chan-wook claims to be his revenge trilogy; the second **Old Boy** (2003) has also been released in the UK. The film's lead Ryu is a deaf

and dumb steelworker who attempts to kidnap the daughter of his boss to pay for a kidney operation that his sister needs. Unsuccessful, Ryu and his girlfriend Cha Yeong-mi, whose idea it was originally, have to then avoid the revenge thirsty boss. Cha (Bae Doo-na of *Take Care of My Cat*) is a political activist, campaigning for the removal of US troops from South Korea. Shin Ha-kyun as Ryu conveys a sophisticated emotional depth without any dialogue, reminiscent of but surpassing the similar role of Kong in the Pang brothers' *Bangkok Dangerous* (2000). *Sympathy for Mr Vengeance* is an extremely brutal and violent film, though not exploitative, and unlike many extreme Asian films, does not underestimate or patronise its audience.

Take Care of My Cat (Goyangileul butaghae)
Dir. Jeong Jae-eun
South Korea 2001 Korean 112m
US/HK/Korean DVD available (seen on UK television)
See above section on *Take Care of My Cat.*

The Isle (Seom)
Dir. Kim Ki-duk
South Korean 2000 Korean 88m
UK DVD available
The Isle received a belated UK release after much controversy around scenes that depict cruelty to fish – and, arguably, women. The BBFC removed just under two minutes from the film, though I would argue strongly for their relevance as the film is about a fishing community and the cruelty acts as a metaphor for the pain the characters inflict on themselves or others. The extremely disturbing scenes of sexual violence remain, however. *The Isle* continues director Kim Ki-duk's obsession with criminals, prostitutes and marginalised people. Hin-jin is a boat keeper who services the local fisherman in several ways including sexually. Her life is changed by the arrival of Hyun-shik, who has come to the isle to commit suicide after killing his girlfriend. The film is a subtle yet shocking study of a relationship between two broken and desperate people.

Select Bibliography
There are far more books on Hong Kong cinema than any of the others, though beware of many of them being fan based rather than scholarly. There are not many books on China's Sixth Generation or

South Korean cinema but do check for new titles being released as a lot of these films are still very new. The majority of books available on mainland Chinese cinema are about the Fifth Generation and earlier so check the contents before buying. Taiwanese cinema is the least written about and Japanese cinema is not included below but there are many easily accessible books. There's still plenty of information to be found on the Internet through the usual search engines.

Books – General

- Berry, Chris. *Chinese Films in Focus: 25 New Takes*. London: BFI Publishing, 2003.
- Hill, J. and Gibson, P. C. (eds). *The Oxford Guide to Film Studies*. Oxford: Oxford University Press, 1998.
- Yang, J. *Once Upon a Time in China: A Guide to Hong Kong, Taiwanese, and Mainland Chinese Cinema*. New York: Atria Books, 2003.

Books – Hong Kong New Wave

- Bordwell, D. *Planet Hong Kong: Popular Cinema and the Art of Entertainment*. London: Harvard University Press, 2000.
- Fu, P. and Desser, D. (eds) *The Cinema of Hong Kong: History, Arts, Identity*. Cambridge: Cambridge University Press, 2000.
- Redmond, S. *Studying Chunking Express*. Leighton Buzzard: Auteur, 2004.
- Stokes, L.O. and Hoover, M. *City on Fire: Hong Kong Cinema*. London: Verso, 1999.
- Teo, S. Hong Kong: *The Extra Dimensions*. London: BFI Publishing, 1997.
- Teo, S. *Wong Kar-Wai*. London: BFI Publishing, 2004.
- Yau, E. (ed.). *At Full Speed: Hong Kong Cinema in a Borderless World*. Minneapolis, MN: University of Minnesota Press, 2001.

Articles

- Doyle, C. 'To the End of the World' in *Sight & Sound*, May 1997.
- Gross, L. 'Nonchalant Grace' in *Sight & Sound*, September 1996.

Books – China's 6 G

- Cornelius, S. *New Chinese Cinema* (Short Cuts Series). London: Wallflower Press, 2001.

Books – South Korean New Wave

- Leong, A. *Korean Cinema: The New Hong Kong*. Trafford Publishing, 2004
- Stringer, J. and Chi-Yun Shin. *New Korean Cinema*. Edinburgh: Edinburgh University Press, 2005.

Internet – General

There are hundreds of websites and putting any film into a search engine such as Google will reveal a hundred more! Not all are useful but only familiarity with the internet will help you sieve through them faster. Here a few suggestions:

- **A Chinese Cinema Page**
  http://www.chinesecinemas.org/
  Articles and reviews, website by Shelly Kraicer.
- **Asianfilms.org http://www.asianfilms.org**
  Dedicated to promoting Chinese, Japanese and Korean film.
- **Bright Lights Film Journal**
  http://www.brightlightsfilm.com/
  Online American Journal with articles on East Asian cinema.
- **Guardian Film Unlimited**
  http://film.guardian.co.uk/
  One of the best UK sites for East Asian film articles.
- **Hong Kong Movie Database**
  http://www.hkmdb.com/
  Information about Hong Kong films, not always up to date.
- **Korean Film Council**
  http://www.koreanfilm.or.kr/
  Promotes Korean films worldwide, includes statistics on industry.
- **Koreanfilm.org http://koreanfilm.org/**
  Site by knowledgeable Korean film specialist Darcy Paquet.

- **Korean Movie Database**
  http://www.hancinema.net
  Information about Korean films, not as detailed as
  IMDB.
- **Internet Movie Database http://www.imdb.com/**
  Extensive film database for films from all countries.
- **Senses of Cinema**
  http://www.sensesofcinema.com/
  Online Australian Film Journal with a large number of
  articles about East Asian cinema.
- **Time Asia http://www.time.com/time/asia/**
  News website for area, some film articles.

Indian
Cinema

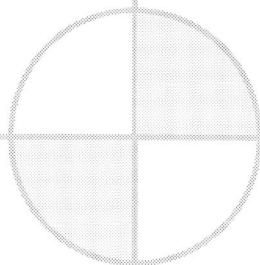

Introduction

The Indian film industry has generally produced near to, or over, 700 feature films annually since the late 1970s. This reached a peak of 948 in 1990. Of these around 200 have been in Hindi (Rajadhyaksha and Willemen 1999: 31-2), many of which represent Indian cinemas most popular form, the Bollywood spectacular. The remainder have been produced in the other languages of the sub-continent, such as Tamil, Telugu, Kannada, Malayalam and Bengali. By any estimation this is an enourmous number of films from a variety of cultural contexts. So, by necessity this teachers' guide to Indian cinema will have to be rather schematic. As Sumita S. Chakravarty argues, 'Indian cinema is too diverse, Indian culture too complex, Indian artistic traditions too varied and eclectic for any one study to encompass their whole range' (1993: 17). Certainly in any introduction of this sort certain generalisations have to be made in order to allow me to discuss the products of one of the most productive film industries in the world and suggest how they might be encompassed within our teaching practices. For ease of use I have therefore divided this chapter of *Alternatives to Hollywood* into two broad sections designed to cover films that are most likely to be utilised by teachers. The first explores what might be labelled Indian art cinema; the second, the popular Hindi film industry, 'Bollywood', a cinema that is becoming increasingly popular outside India. Towards the end of this section I will offer short case studies of a number of Indian films which have had a significant impact with audiences around the world. I will end by suggesting a number of ways in which these exciting and exhilirating films may be used with students.

Art Cinema in India

Not surprisingly, the first Indian films to receive international attention were what can be broadly defined as 'art' movies, as these works fit the tastes of the international art house audience. Gokulsing and Dissanayake argue that these works are distinguished by the fact that they are 'realistic, often ethnographic and seek to capture important aspects of Indian reality' (1998: 30). These films received distribution outside India, particularly at prestigious international film festivals. This exposure led to their being shown in art house cinemas, film societies and University film clubs in the West. Their often earnest nature makes them particularly suited to the approaches adopted by serious film critics. Indian art films contrast sharply with the popular output of other types of film-making, particularly the Hindi popular cinema associated with Mumbai.

Defining art cinema

Art cinema is often loosely defined as those films that are exhibited outside the mainstream. This is often linked to the idea that they are not simply commercially produced films, but wish to engage with social issues and conditions. David Bordwell in his 'The Art Cinema as a Mode of Film Practice' strives to make a clear formal distinction between art cinema and classical narrative cinema. He argues that it appears after the Second World War as Hollywood's dominance was beginning to wane and international film production began again in earnest (1979: 56). For Bordwell, the art film is marked by three important elements: a concern with realism, authorship and ambiguity. He sees as central a different approach to narrative, 'the art cinema defines itself explicitly against the classical narrative mode, and especially against the cause and effect linkage of events' (ibid.: 57). Bordwell argues that the idea of realism is often evoked in relation to art cinema, mainly due to the use of real locations rather than studio sets and its addressing real problems, worked out through psychologically rounded and complex characters. He puts it thus, 'the characters of the art cinema lack defined desires and goals. Characters may act for inconsistent reasons or may question themselves about their goals. Choices are vague or non-existent. Hence a certain drifting episodic quality to the art film's narrative' (ibid.: 58).

Bordwell also argues that 'the art cinema foregrounds the author as a structure in the film's system: the author becomes a formal component, the overriding intelligence organizing the film for our comprehension' (ibid.: 59). This is always linked to the assumption that the art film director is able to achieve a higher degree of artistic freedom, which in turn allows them to follow through their unique artistic vision. The lack of star performers in the art film means that the director is the figure that unifies the text. Such films are not concluded in a straightforward way and the ambiguity of the endings of many art films operates to highlight the fact that there are no easy conclusions to the situations shown. It also encourages critics to see every work by an art film director as part of a body of work, each offering itself 'as a chapter in an ouevre" (ibid.: 59). This, in turn, privileges the position of the critic who may present themselves as one of the few who can place each work into this context and hence interpret it 'correctly'. Bordwell's work enables us to begin to tie down what an art film might actually be. Certainly, in the context of Indian cinema much of what he says is applicable. Art cinema is seen as more artistic, realistic and complex than that produced within the commercial sphere, Bollywood.

Typical of the assertions and distinctions made by critics is the work of John W. Hood. Indeed, his *The Essential Mystery: Major Flmmakers of the Indian Art Cinema* (2000) is replete with assumptions about the value of art cinema and the limits of commercial films. He argues that:

> What can be most easily discerned about modern Indian art cinema is what it is not. It clearly lacks the major characteristics of the commercial cinema; songs and dances, titillating sexual suggestiveness, the representation of violence as entertaining, melodrama and the narrative predictability of established formula. More positively, art cinema is free to experiment with form, style and structure. (2000: 5)

In this conception of art cinema, and indeed in much critical writing about Indian cinema, one name recurs more than any other. He is a director who made films that are seen by many as the epitome of art cinema, Satyajit Ray.

Satyajit Ray and Indian art cinema

Ray was born in Calcutta in 1912. It was there that he was a key contributor to the establishment of the Calcutta Film Society in 1947. This introduced him to a range of European cinemas (their first screening was Eisenstein's **Battleship Potemkin**, 1925) and to the possibilities of film-making outside the Hollywood model . In an article for the 'Statesman' he made this clear:

> It should be realised that the average American film is a bad model because it depicts a way of life which is utterly at variance with our own. Moreover the high technical polish which is the hallmark of the standard Hollywood product would be impossible to achieve under existing Indian conditions. What India needs today is not more gloss, but more imagination, more integrity, and more intelligent appreciation of the limitations of the medium. (quoted in Ray 1997: 14)

When Jean Renoir was in India during 1949 to make **The River** (1951) he had a further, significant impact on how Ray thought films should be made. Ray accompanied the French director on his location hunts and used the time to discuss cinema with him. These trips planted the seeds that would grow into Ray's first film. When he later saw the Italian neo-realist classic **Bicycle Thieves** (1948) during a visit to London, it confirmed the idea that he could actually make his first film, **Pather Panchali** (1955). It was the Italian film's use of non-actors, its lack of make-up, its location shooting and its use of poor film stock that contributed to his new conviction that he too could make such as film (Ray 1997: 25). Through his film viewing Ray was able to draw on a range of stylistic influences. Roy Armes has observed that 'it is important to remember that his work has no roots in the traditions of Indian film making. Thus, though Ray was deeply influenced by Indian culture through his studies at Santineketan, he was largely Western in his film tastes' (1987: 232). Not for him the world of the Hindi song and dance cinema. However, it would be wrong to suggest that his films are in some way un-Indian, they are concretely set within the context of a changing India. His style of film-making may be more easily accessible to western audiences, particularly those patrons of the festival and art house circuits. Hence, for many audiences over 35 years, the name of Satyajit Ray became synonymous with art cinema from India.

Pather Panchali tells the story of a young child, Apu, growing up in a Bengali village. The film unfolds events in his family and their neighbours lives, always seen or reflected through the youngster's eyes. These events – some are every day, such as visiting merchants and theatrical players, while some more momentous, such as the death through fever of his sister Durga – all develop in a simple way with a slow pace. The film

© BFI Stills

Character is the central focus to Ray's early films, such as **Pather Panchali**

contrasts sharply with the codes and conventions of mainstream Hindi popular cinema and has often been labelled 'pure' cinema.

The opening of the film makes these differences clear suggesting **Pather Panchali**, if we use Bordwell's definitions, is clearly an 'art film'. At the start of the film Durga steals some fruit from a neighbour's orchard, then wanders back through the forest. From the outset we are presented with an everyday occurrence. However, the films refuses to set up a mainstream enigma style narrative. There is no clear resort to the logic of cause and effect as Durga skips through the forest back to her family home. Here we are conscious that the film is made on location. The shots are in fairly long takes and there seems to be little of the dynamism one would expect of mainstream narrative cinema. The use of location and the slow pace of the opening suggest a work interested in realism rather than spectacle. It also suggests the film is concerned with character rather than action. We are introduced to Durga, her mother, the neighbours and auntie very simply. Characters are presented as real people rather than the functional roles they may have assumed in a more conventional work. They, along with the character of Apu, form the centre of the film. When Durga returns to the family home there are a number of long takes as she goes about her business in the courtyard. She moves in and out of the static frame, as Ray once again attempts to create a sense of realism. The actor performs in front of the camera but the effect is one that suggests the character is being observed by the camera. However, in among these we have shots, such as the famous one where Durga looks into the pot that contains her kittens, that clearly cry out that they have been carefully constructed. Authorship becomes apparent in among the realism. Thus, from the outset *Pather Panchali* may be considered an art film as it fits much of the criteria Bordwell puts forward. Not surprisingly then it was well received in international circles, with champions of the Indian art film such as John W. Hood calling it 'a masterpiece' (2000: 53). Ray would establish himself as an art house auteur, someone whose work needed to be read as a body if one element is to be fully understood, by completing a trilogy of films about Apu with *Aparajito* (1956) and *The World of Apu* (1959).

Funding Art Cinema

The production of *Pather Panchali* received some financial assistance from the government of West Bengal, and such official sources would play an important part in the development of the art cinema that followed Ray's debut. Some of Ray's later films, such as *Nayak* (1966), would find financial support from the Film Finance Corporation (FFC). The latter was set up in 1960 under the control of the Ministry of Finance. By 1964 control had passed onto the Ministry of Information and Broadcasting. It was under their tutelage that the funding of cinema began to focus on particular types of film. They assisted in the production of Mrinal Sen's *Bhuvan Shome* (1969), which many argue ushered in what has become known as 'New Indian Cinema' or 'Parallel Cinema'. By 1971 the Corporation declared that it aimed to 'develop the film in India into an effective instrument for the promotion of national culture, education and healthy entertainment by granting loans for modest but off-beat films of talented and promising people in the field' (quoted in Rayadhyaksha and Willemen 1998: 162). This clearly meant films produced outside the commercial structures of India's mainstream cinema. In 1980 the FFC was merged with the Film Export Corporation to create the much larger National Film Development Corporation (NFDC). However, they failed to develop a distribution infrastructure for these 'new' films, which in the long run would have serious consequences for this sector of the Indian film industry. In particular as television took over as the primary provider of material for the audience that had patronised the Parallel Cinema.

Parallel Cinema

The label 'Parallel Cinema' was coined by journalist Arvind Mehta. It quickly became the accepted label for films that rejected the commercial film industries of India, and in particular Mumbai. Mehta saw 'Parallel Cinema' as one that 'could co-exist in a parallel trajectory to popular cinema' (Datta 2002: 25). This cinema was based on the aesthetics of realism, telling tales that explored the experiences of the poor and marginalised in society. As the term parallel suggests, film-makers working within this sphere did not include the staples of the commercial industry such as star names, spectacle and excess, and song and dance routines. As Datta puts it:

> *The new cinema film-makers turned away from formulaic, sentimentalised melodrama, from the pleasures of spectacle as in song and dance, and action, and from mandatory happy endings. Adapting the realistic aesthetic, they cast new actors with no glamour attached to play recognisable characters in a specific milieu. Following the European neo-realists, they opted out of the studio environments and set their narratives in realistic settings – in most cases, rural locales. (2002: 35)*

At the centre of these films was a concern with experimentation in terms of form, technique and the language of cinema. They rejected the idea that film simply reproduced successful formulas. Thompson and Bordwell link the work of directors associated with Parallel Cinema to other film movements that appeared in the 1960s. They specifically evoke post-war Italian cinema and the Czech New Wave when they state that 'most represented quiet social commentary, influenced by Ray's humanistic realism, Italian neo-realism, and European new cinemas' (2003: 641).

One of the most stridently political film-makers to come to prominence in this period was Mrinal Sen. According to Thompson and Bordwell Sen became known for his political critique in works such as *The Interview* (1971), which cast an unemployed worker in the central role of an unemployed middle class man seeking a job. The political concerns of the director surface once again in *Calcutta '71*(1972) which offers five case studies of poverty within the city and criticises parlimentary democracy as it does. Sen carefully constructs stories that show the inequalities he saw in Indian society of the time, each heavily informed by his left wing ideals. He continued this critique with his *Chorus* (1974), which attacks multi-national companies and their exploitation of India.

Mrinal Sen: his work expressed his left wing world view

Throughout his work, Thompson and Bordwell argue Sen 'experimented with stylized performance, Brechtian reflexivity, direct address to the audience, and other tactics of political modernism' (2003: 641). In this respect Sen's work may be linked to the overtly modernist and political works of 1960s European directors such as Antonioni and Godard rather than the more humanist models such as Renoir who had inspired Ray. Sen stated that the films of Antonioni are 'very much my cup of tea...Ray and I differ regarding *La notte* (1961), which he sees as pessimistic. I think it is rather optimistic...Antonioni is ruthlessly analytical, like Henry James. And he is still also a Marxist, as he scrutinises through man-woman relations the various strata of the middle class' (Williams 2000: 18-19). However, Sen also had an allegiance with film-makers from the third world and the movement known as Third Cinema. This was an overtly political film movement that rejected the gloss of Hollywood cinema and other national cinemas that followed Hollywood's mode of film production. The fact that Sen was 'doggedly committed to an art cinema ethos' (Chakavarty 2000: 1) was linked to his politicised views. This meant that he produced films that interogated both the structures of Indian (particularly Calcutta) society, the film's subject matter, as well as the way in which film represented the world (the form of the film). Sen's films therefore are not always easy viewing but they do offer the opportunity to consider the ways in which some non-Hollywood film-makers have attempted to offer different ways of representing the world. In this way Sen is a useful director to compare with post-1968 Godard and the Dziga Vertov collective as their aims and methods have many similarities. Sen offers a model of Indian film-making that rejects the representations of mainstream popular cinema.

Conclusion

In *The Essential Mystery*, Hood links the creativity of the Indian art film directors, such as Ray and those associated with Parallel Cinema, with the endeavours of other artists such as writers, poets and painters. For many years western audiences were only able to see art films produced in India as they were the only films that received any level of distribution. This tells us as much about critics and writers such as Hood as it does about the films and directors they choose to champion. Hood has clear expectations of what 'good' film-making is about, and that is certainly not about entertainment. It is these kinds of perspectives among critics writing about non-Hollywood cinema that has marginalised the popular or commercial films of industries such as India. In the UK that popular cinema has now become much better known for a number of significant reasons.

Popular Hindi film: 'Bollywood'

Popular Hindi films have a special place in current British culture. Screenings of the latest Bollywood blockbusters consistently fill cinemas throughout the UK. The BBC has a Bollywood number as one of its programme links, and Comic Relief chose to 'Bollywoodise' the video for 'Spirit in the Sky', one of its charity singles. Bollywood is everywhere.

It is also possible to argue that the popularity of Bollywood films represents the last bastion of real family film-going in the UK. Attend any screening and it is likely it will be filled by people of all ages. Bollywood produces films that appeal to different generations as opposed to many Hollywood 'kids' films which see parents being dragged along to cinemas simply because their youngsters want to watch them. Indeed, the potential of Bollywood at the UK box-office was confirmed with the release of ***Kabhi Khushi Kabhie Gham*** (also known as ***3KG***) during December 2001, which saw it enter the UK box-office charts at number 3, just behind the more traditional family fare, ***Harry Potter*** and the Samuel L. Jackson vehicle ***The 51st***

State. The latest Bollywood releases are now regularly appearing in the UK box-office top 10. Bollywood, a term that was once seen as derogatory and dismissive has now become accepted, even embraced, as people become more aware of popular Hindi cinema. Here I want to introduce the key elements of Bollywood cinema formula.

The Bollywood Formula

Ravi S. Vasudevan (2000: 134) has noted that popular Hindi cinema was dismissed 'for its derivativeness from American cinema, the melodramatic externality and stereotyping of its characters, and especially for its failure to focus on the psychology of human interaction'. Rosie Thomas also acknowledges this and goes on to suggest the ways in which popular Indian cinema, Bollywood, has often been dismissed by critics in the West. She outlines the ways in which they see many of these popular films as, to put it bluntly, not really worth taking seriously, arguing that in their responses such critics often tend to offer a number of well-established clichés, 'the films are said to be nightmarishly lengthy, second-rate copies of Hollywood trash, to be dismissed with patronising amusement or facetious quips' (1985: 117). However, as Film Studies acknowledges the importance of popular cinemas from around the world, Bollywood is taking its place as an industry worthy of detailed and sustained critical interest. The recent explosion of critical work devoted to Bollywood reflects this, and offers teachers a body of work to draw on in the classroom.

Non-realist traditions

Like other popular cinemas from across the world, Indian popular cinema does not always rely heavily on western models of realism. This has created problems for some critics, who traditionally have associated attempts at 'realism' with seriousness. In particular, they have dismissed the films because of their non-naturalistic narrative patterns and storylines, and their reliance upon repetition within their formula. However, it is possible to argue that these 'problems' for some may also be seen as interesting challenges to the dominant western models of film-making. As Thomas notes, the lack of clear storyline can be explained in the context of Indian cinema:

> What is meant by 'no story' is, first, that the story-line will be almost totally predictable to the Indian audience, being a repetition, or rather, an unmistakable transformation, of many

other Hindi films, and second, that it will be recognised by
them as a 'ridiculous' pretext for spectacle and emotion. (1985:
123)

The cultural traditions of the sub-continent mean that originality is not always the most valued element in what a film has to offer to an audience.

Elements of the Bollywood Formula

Gokulsing and Dissanayake, in their useful book Indian *Popular Cinema: A Narrative of Cultural Change* (1998), acknowledge the centrality of formula, offering the following list of elements:

> *Indian popular films are not realistic in the strictest sense.*
> *They seek to create a world of fantasy.*
> *Acting is exaggerated.*
> *All aspects of the filmic experience are melodramatic.*
> *The use of the camera is often flashy, drawing attention to*
> *itself.*
> *Editing is very obtrusive.*
> *Stereotypes related to character and situation are common.*
> *Music is central.*
> *Songs, very often sung by well-known playback singers, are*
> *crucial in unfolding the narrative.*
> *Dance sequences are often used to intensify the intended*
> *emotions and the spectacle. (1998: 95)*

Of course, like any cinematic set of codes and conventions these change historically and are open to the influence of wider shifts in cultural trends. For example, the big blockbusters of the 1970s such as **Sholay** (1975) contained less songs than the popular romantic melodramas of the 1950s and 1960s. The hits of the 1990s have increased the level of spectacle on offer to audiences.

Excess and Spectacle

Thomas (1985) also develops the idea of the formula of the Bollywood film when she too suggests that there are a number of elements that can be argued are central to the Bollywood movie. As such films are designed to appeal to large audiences, who have certain expectations of this cinema, they will seek to deliver these elements to them. Sometimes this will involve a reworking or refiguring of familiar components. Bollywood films operate in an excessive manner and a crucial part of the escapism, so important to the Hindi blockbuster, is their willingness to present their stories in a larger than life, almost fantastic way. Thomas also suggests that 'spectacular and emotional excess will invariably be privileged over linear narrative development' (1985: 124). This excess is linked to another key element, spectacle. Again Thomas argues that spectacle is one of the things that are essential to the continued mass appeal of Bollywood films, 'song and dance, locations, costumes, fights and thrills (or stunts), most of Bombay's top stars' (ibid.). In the examples explored below it is possible to identify how these key components subtly change over time to ensure the continued popularity of Bollywood cinema.

Narratives

Thomas goes on to argue that there are also certain narratives that are typical within Hindi popular cinema and that these narrative components are used again and again. Once more this reveals how the formula of Bollywood can change over time while still using the narrative structures audiences are familiar with and desire. For example, in the 1970s and 1980s many films, such as the Amitabh Bachchan star vehicle *Muqaddar Ka Sikandar* (1978), incorporated stories of children being lost and found, revenge for wrongs, and two male friends falling in love with the same woman often leading to a significant sacrifice based on love. All these narrative twists can be found in the popular films of earlier decades. However, in the 1970s and 1980s they were given a much tougher, urban edge. Such films usually revolved around fate, destiny and issues of duty and kinship, and familiar narratives were worked and reworked throughout a series of films. Again, as Thomas suggests, this means that we can assume the audiences for Bollywood films don't concern themselves overly with things such as originality of plot, and are much more interested in the ways that the films present and explore expected plot twists. For Bollywood audiences then excess and spectacle take priority over narrative originality, with audiences looking for a visually spectacular presentation of a film's story and themes. Part of this celebration of excess is central to the element most people are most familiar with, the musical, or song and dance, number.

Song and Dance

The song and dance number is a central element of the formula of any Bollywood movie. Indeed, Shah Rukh Khan has commented that if *Gladiator* (2000) had been made in Mumbai it would have contained songs. These song and dance numbers usually reflect the emotional content of the film, as Thomas argues 'Hindi film songs are usually tightly integrated, through words and mood, within the flow of the film' (1985: 127). More recently, however, while they have remained an integral element in the films themselves, they have increasingly become part of the wider marketing strategies employed by distributors to market their new releases. Song and dance numbers are routinely taken out of films and used on the popular Indian cable and satellite music channels in the build up to a film's release. This has the effect of heightening the public's awareness of the film and its stars. Because of their use in this context it is possible to see the visual influence of pop music videos on an aesthetic level. As Gokulsing and Dissanayake argue, 'the impact of western musical television (MTV) is being increasingly felt in Indian films: their pace, the camera angles, the music, the dance sequences' (1998: 95). In contemporary Bollywood movies songs are also often used to unlock their audiences knowledge of other Hindi films and so create a nostalgic celebration of the form. This undoubtedly reflects the cultural importance of Bollywood for, particularly, NRI (non-resident Indians) audiences throughout the diaspora. For example, in *Kabhi Khushi Kabhie Gham* , 'Aati Kya Khandala', from the 1998 hit film *Ghulam*, is used, as well as refrains from older, familiar film songs such as 'Vande Mataram' and 'Jana Gana Mana'.

The 1990s to the Present

A key film, and one that represents some of the most significant shifts in the 1990s, is Sooraj Barjatya's *Hum Aapke Hain Koun...!* (1994). It contains some of the changes that would be consolidated by a number of hugely successful films that followed its new take on the blockbuster formula to box-office success in the years that followed. *Hum Aapke Hain Koun...!* privileges romance over action, contains more numbers than the 1970s blockbusters and starred rising stars of the Hindi film industry, in this case, Madhuri Dixit and Salaman Khan. One of the most popular films ever at the Indian box-office, it seemed to re-centre family values and the family audience after the action and revenge dramas associated with the Bachchan star persona, offering little that might be considered controversial. According to Rajadhyaksha and Willemen (1999: 519), the film is a remake of the 1982 box-office failure *Nadiya Ke Paar*, perhaps revealing how much the tastes of audiences had changed in the period between the two versions of the story.

However, the film that most clearly shows the shift towards an interest in non-resident Indians, in terms of both subject matter and potential audience is *Dilwale Dulhania Le Jayenge* (1995). A massive hit which, according to Anupama Chopra, holds the record for continuous exhibition in India (2002: 8). The film opens with Amrish Puri playing a newsagent who has been resident in London for 22 years, feeding the pigeons in Trafalgar Square. In a voice-over he explains how he feels he has been chained to this place by his economic circumstances and that one day he plans to return home to the Punjab. He closes his eyes and the films first song and dance number begins with a group of women wearing colourful clothing dancing in a field. This memory of the Punjab corresponds with Hindi popular cinemas representations of the place. From the outset the nostalgic representation of the Punjab is presented unquestioningly as 'truthful'. The opening gives authority to the mythical 'India' created by the film industry. Versions of this mythical India have become more commonplace in some of the most recent blockbusters such as *Mohabbatein* (2000) and *Kabhi Khushi Kabhie Gham* as they strive to represent an acceptable vision of 'home'. The opening sequence continues with a crane down to reveal Puri in a field in front of the dancers still feeding the birds. The positioning of the actor within his character's fantasy also works to position his vision of a rural experience as particularly 'authentic'. This might explain the films popularity with urban Indian audiences who are invited to see their 'home' in this idyllic pre-industrial rural world. Somewhere that does not evoke the corruption of the city or rather its cinematic representation, in particular those from urban set films from the 1970s onwards. The lyrics of the song work to reinforce these visual ideas, 'come home stranger, your country calls you'. The fantasy of rural bliss is shattered by the bells of St. Martins in the Field, a typically British sound, which drown out the sound of the song. This is followed by a montage of Puri walking around London to his workplace under the credits. The settings are shot in a way that highlights their dullness and he carries an Umbrella, which he has to use. Again, this is edited in a way that contrasts his reality in Britain with his colourful vision of the Punjab. *Dilwale Dulhania Le Jayenge* marks an important move towards the creation of a mythical India in popular Hindi films that, it might be argued, is constructed as much for those outside India as those within.

By 1998 these family orientated films had retaken the box-office. Controversial films still found an audience, such as *Roja* (1992), which looked at a terrorist kidnapping in Kashmir, and **Bombay** (1995) which focused on the relationship between a Muslim woman and a Hindu man against the backdrop of urban religious riots. Both of these films were directed by Mani Ratnam, who was best known for working in the Tamil industry and for many epitomises the socially conscious popular film-maker. Other films proved controversial as they reflected the changing approaches to issues such as sex, for example, **Khalnayak** (1993) which contained the number 'Choli Ke Peechay', performed by Madhuri Dixit and asking the question, what is beneath my veil, what is under my blouse?'.

Typical of the shift back to romantic storylines in the 1990s is the mega-hit **Kuch Kuch Hota Hai** (1998). This is a film that clearly aspires to and achieves blockbuster status. It is a useful example here as it clearly shows a number of important developments in the Hindi blockbuster of the period, while still offering the key components of melodrama, romance, spectacle, exotic locations, comedy, and song and dance. On a basic level the production values on display here are much higher than the blockbusters from the 70s and early 80s. The camera work, editing and sound are all much more polished than was present in earlier decades. This of course can be explained to some degree by technological advances and higher budgets. Like other romantic films of the mid-1990s, **Kuch Kuch Hota Hai** contains more songs than the more action driven, male orientated films of the 70s and 80s. Here there are 12, and they are shot in a more flamboyant style, clearly directed towards the demands of satellite channels and influenced by music video aesthetics as discussed above.

More significantly there is a much greater focus on women. Rather than being the tale of two men who fall in love with the same woman that leads to sacrifice, **Kuch Kuch Hota Hai** presents two women who love the same man. One of them, Anjali, is the character who makes the sacrifice, leaving Rhaul and Tina to fall in love and marry. The film also reveals a more general shift away from engaging with contemporary social issues, in particular class, which had been so emblematic of the Bachchan films of the 70s and 80s. Here the main characters are young university students, care-free and clearly very middle class. This is revealed through the designer clothes: DKNY, GAP, Polo, Speedo, etc., that make up their costumes. The only worry there seems to be in their life is who to fall in love with. The central characters offer models of aspiration for audiences rather than the identification of films that focused on lower class characters. The world of the **Kuch Kuch Hota Hai** is one of fantasy, but here the fantasy is one that is unattainable rather than the earlier fantasies of justice that mark the Bachchan films. This element is also reflected in the use of Scottish locations, that create an unworldly setting that does not correspond to the real life experiences of the audience.

Kabhi Khushi Kabhie Gham: reaching diasporic audiences

Over the past few years Bollywood was touted in the British media as the next movie cross-over phenomenon. This followed the massive international success of Ang Lee's mandarin language *Crouching Tiger, Hidden Dragon* (2000) which suggested a substantial potential market for subtitled films in the UK. In 2001, foreign language Oscar contender *Lagaan* and the Shah Rukh Kahn produced *Ashoka* were both critically well received in the mainstream UK media and did reasonably well at the box-office. However, the film that really attracted large audiences was much more typical of certain trends in the contemporary Hindi blockbuster. *Kabhi Khushi Kabhie Gham* is a large scale, star filled, love story. Perhaps the most significant part of its blockbuster status is the fact that it represents the shift towards creating films that are no longer simply aimed at the indigenous Indian market, but actively seek audiences within the South Asian diaspora. In particular those residing in the UK, Canada and the US. This is not surprising when one considers that the audience outside India can account for around 65% of a film's total earnings (Banker 2001: 8). Unlike *Crouching Tiger, Hidden Dragon* the primary market for *Kabhi Khushi Kabhie Gham* in the UK was drawn from the diasporic community. It would be wrong to see the success of this film as needing any cross-over into the subtitled market. As the box-office returns for non-subtitled screenings of Hindi language films in the UK is substantial.

One of the main elements that reflects these shifts is the creation, on screen, of a mythical India. One which appeals to the nostalgic feelings in the diasporic audience. This serves an important function for young and old Asians in Britain. This is highlighted by the reasons often offered for attending screenings of Hindi films. For example, when Hyphen Films conducted a series of interviews for their introductions to Channel 4's *Bollywood Best* season, screened in the summer of 2001, many people reflected upon why they thought that Hindi popular cinema is important for non-resident Indians. One young woman in Birmingham, for example, stated that 'growing up in

England we need something to remind us of our culture and stuff. Indian films are good at that.' Her reflections were reinforced by a young man, also in Birmingham, who explained why he liked visiting the cinema to see Indian films, 'a lot of Indian people, like myself, come to see Indian films basically to see our culture. We get to see parts of India, to see some rituals that perhaps we don't perform here anymore, but we do still back home. Ultimately we are Indian and we still have things in common with people from India, and when we see things on the screen we feel closer to home.' It is these feelings and desires that the newest type of Hindi blockbuster seems specifically designed to cater for. For example, *Kabhi Khushi Kabhie Gham* involves characters who are displaced to the UK, due to a family fall out, but hold on to their values drawn from India and their being Indian. The characters' dialogue seems almost written in a way that is calculated to appeal to NRIs and other emigrant communities from the sub-continent. The elements that constitute the Hindi blockbuster have slowly shifted and developed over the past ten years in ways that allow the inclusion of material that will appeal to audiences in India but also, crucially, abroad.

Case Studies

Contemporary Bollywood: *Mohabbatein* (Aditya Chopra, 2000)

As noted, the enormous success of the more romantically orientated family films of the late 1990s marked a significant shift in the make up of the Hindi blockbuster. Romantic stories mixed with comic sub-plots became the dominant narrative structure. An excellent example of this style is *Mohabbatein*. Released in 2000, the film appears to have been conceived as a blockbuster. Three young men arrive at the famous Gurukul university which operates within a strict set of rules which forbids them contact with the outside world. Despite this each meets and falls in love with a young woman. A new music teacher, Raj, arrives at the university and teaches them the importance of following their heart. The film is cast to appeal across the generations. One of the most popular stars of the late 1990s, Shahrukh Khan plays the new teacher and appears alongside Hindi blockbuster legend, Amitabh Bachchan, who plays the old fashioned university principal. The battle between the world view of these characters is at the moral centre of the film, and the bringing together of these two enormous stars is a strategy familiar from the multi-starrer films of the 1970s and 80s. Here the main difference is the generation gap, and this can be viewed as a strategy to appeal to different elements of the mass, mainstream audience which will be consist of different generations. However, Bachchan's presence might also be designed to appeal to those outside India who still see him as the epitome of the Hindi film star. If, as argued earlier through the example of interviews with young British Asians, non-resident Indian's experience of India and its culture is filtered through cinema images then films wishing to appeal to that audience would logically include the iconic figure of Bachchan. As 'real' memories of 'home' are replaced by cinematic images, both Bachchan and the place he occupies within popular culture become even more important.

There are other elements in the film that contribute to its status as a blockbuster. The film has seven songs with music written by the team behind the successful **Kuch Kuch Hota Hai**, Jatin-Lalit. Setting the film in a university also reflects an attempt to repeat the formula of the earlier, enormously popular, film. What is striking in this case is the use of English locations, in particular, Oxford University and Longleat House which is used for Gurukul University. The sheer size of the film suggests the shifts in the Hollywood blockbuster in the early 1960s when producers were forever trying to top the films that had been successful before with bigger, more spectacular products. Here everything has the feel of being calculated to be bigger and more spectacular and impressive than earlier blockbusters. For example, replacing the one central romantic story of earlier films with the triple story of the young students and their search for love.

Intertextuality and contemporary Bollywood

Another striking feature of the film is the level of intertextuality. Again, something that had been creeping into Hindi popular cinema since the 1970s. Early in **Mohabbatein** there are two moments that clearly reflect this trend and celebrate Hindi popular cinema and the audiences knowledge of it. First, the introductory appearance of Bachchan as the strict principal, Shankar. As the young men look out of their bedroom window they see a figure, cloaked and standing next to a lake in the university grounds. The camera tracks towards him from the back as he looks toward the rising sun. This movement is inter-cut with a close-up of his hands and a close-up of his mouth, followed by a large close-up of his eyes. These are the eyes that are so familiar to most Hindi cinema-goers as they were a trademark of earlier Bachchan films. By this point a Bollywood conscious audience knows who it is. There is then a cut as he turns towards the camera in slow motion and throws his cloak over his shoulder and begins to walk. This scene dramatically introduces the character through clever use of the audience's awareness of the actor and the seriousness of his status within Indian popular culture. Indeed, his character is someone who has to come to terms with a changing world much as the actor himself has had to adapt to playing much older characters as he aged and no longer took the action roles of his heyday. The values he is most closely associated with as a star are no longer central to Hindi popular cinema and this role seems to be aware of this shift in his stardom. The music that accompanies his introduction is sombre and serious compared with the light romantic fare that dominates the rest of the film. Indeed, Bachchan himself commented upon the character, 'He will have to change. The old generation will have to change their old traditions, so that a new generation can create a new tradition,' in a manner that reflects the changes in the Hindi blockbuster, and his place within them.

Shortly after this the second significant intertextual moment occurs. The comic sub-plot in *Mohabbatein* focuses on the attempts of cafe owner Kake to woo Preeto. In the introduction to these characters he sings the romantic theme song to the mega-hit *Kuch Kuch Hota Hai*. Again, this is a clear invitation to the audience to celebrate their knowledge of popular cinema and the songs that they all know. The use of this refrain so early in the film also works as a guarantor to the audience that *Mohabbatein* is aiming to deliver the same sort of romantic, family entertainment provided by the earlier hit.

Class and aspiration in Bollywood today

Mohabbatein also reveals how issues that are central to the film are channelled through individuals rather than through class as in the Bachchan films of the earlier era. It can be argued that this shift is made apparent in the fantasy settings of these later films. *Mohabbatein* uses English locations for the University;

Kuch Kuch Hota Hai uses Scottish ones. Again, as noted earlier, this contrasts with the films of the 70s and 80s which offered audiences recognisable environments within which their stories unfold. The more recent hits create a fantasy world, that through the use of non-Indian locations, does not correspond to a social reality. The socially recognisable settings have now been replaced with ones that highlight the fantasy of the films. Of course, not all Hindi popular cinema follows this model, but it is possible to argue that the blockbuster of the early twenty-first century is moving more and more in this direction. Indeed, one might observe that the formula for success now demands it. However, as always this formula will slowly change. Whatever direction the Hindi popular cinema has taken, these films are now enormously sophisticated pieces of film-making that deliver popular entertainment to audiences all over the globe. As such, they are undoubtedly among the most watched films ever produced by any film industry in the world.

Film Stars: Amitabh Bachchan

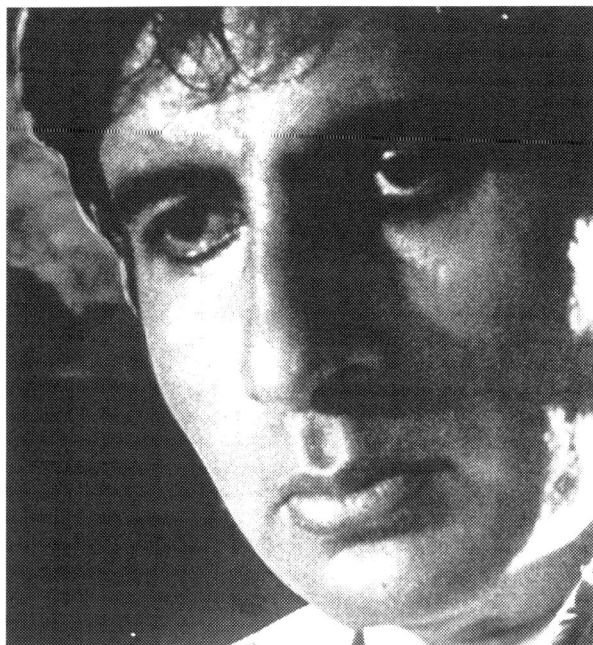

Amitabh Bachchan: for many the epitome of the Hindi film star.

Another of the key factors within Bollywood, as in other popular national cinemas, is stardom and stars are a vital component of any Bollywood spectacular. Indeed, so much so that they often contain more than one big star, their presence vigorously used to assist the promotion and marketing of new films. *Sholay* is certainly reflective of Bollywood's use of stars in the 1970s and is very typical of some of the changes that were occurring at that time. As Arnold notes, 'a change of direction transformed the romantic song and dance extravaganza into the violent, action-packed thriller' (cited in Gokulsing and Dissanayake 1998: 111). *Sholay* is perhaps the most typical and well known example of such changes. It is action-orientated, containing scenes of great energy and spectacle. The film's central characters are anti-heroes whose actions are dictated by notions of honour rather than legality, and who operate on the margins of the criminal world. The film presents these characters in a sympathetic way suggesting that they may have been forced into illegal actions due to the social inequalities they have encountered during their lives. It is also a film that combines more than one star, here Amitabh Bachchan and Dharmendra, in what had by that time become known as 'multi-starrers'. In the mid-1970s and early 1980s one cornerstone of such Hindi blockbusters was Bachchan, the undisputed superstar of Indian cinema and an actor whose mere appearance guaranteed box-office success. His status and presence within the Indian film the industry makes him worthy of further consideration below.

Many of the most typical elements of Bollywood in the mid-1970s and early 80s can be found in his films. Variously referred to as a 'one man film industry', he was by far the biggest attraction in Indian popular cinema of the period. Indeed, Bachchan became so omnipresent within Indian culture that he is often referred to in terms that reflect the intertextual nature of his stardom (Sharma 1993). This is particularly the case in relation to his 1981 hit *Silsila*, which drew on gossip about his private life, casting both his wife Jaya and alleged lover Reka. Another example of Bachchan's enormous presence in the Indian popular imagination is the coverage in the popular media of his on-set injury during the filming of 1983s *Coolie*. Indeed this incident was so much a part of the film that when the final cut was made it included a freeze frame that indicated the stunt that went wrong during a fight scene and accompanied it with text that explained that the star had almost been killed at this point. Certainly this indicates that audiences came to this film with pre-existing knowledge of the star and his accident. Indeed, the finished film itself became an example of his heroic status as he had managed to complete it, and the accident contributed to its success.

As noted above, what is striking about Bachchan from the mid-1970s is how he became an integral part of many large scale blockbusters. However, it would be dangerous to suggest that his presence was the only reason that these films were successful at the box-office. It is worth noting, as Justin Wyatt (1994) does in relation to Hollywood high-concept films of the 1990s, that big stars usually have to appear in the right vehicles, ones that reflect the public's notion of their stardom. Bachchan managed to do this throughout the late 1970s and early 1980s appearing in action, romances and comedies, but he was not the only component in his blockbusters of the period. For example, a very typical Bachchan film is *Amar Akbar Anthony* (1977). It is a good example of the 'multi-starrer', as it showcases the talents of Rishi Kapoor, Vinod Khanna and Parveen Babi as well as Bachchan, and contains a number of storylines, each devoted to one of the stars. Basically three brothers are separated when children and brought up not knowing each other, one by a Christian priest, one by a Muslim tailor and one by a Hindu police officer; these narrative strands are drawn together as the film moves towards its celebratory climax.

The final dance number in the film represents a familiar, ideologically optimistic tendency within Hindi popular cinema. The three brothers unite to save Anthony's girlfriend from a forced marriage to one of the evil Robert's henchmen. They appear in disguises, Anthony as a Catholic priest, Akbar as a tailor and Amar as a one man band. The way in which they manage to forget their religious differences to work together is significant in a continent where religious differences had been marked in recent history. The finale also clearly shows that while the number of songs present in such films may have been reduced their importance is not necessarily any less. The final song represents the coming together of the characters and their backgrounds, the reuniting of the brothers separated by a mixture of a cruel twist of fate and urban poverty. It is absolutely integrated into the overall structure of the film and is certainly not an additional sidebar to the narrative and ideological drive of the film. Indeed, the plea for unity visually represented by the song is made all the more effective because of its articulation within such a celebratory moment. The dance movements of the three male leads (e.g. they walk up stairs in unison with their hands on each other's shoulders), and their singing in harmony reveal how the integration is realised within the actual cinematic construction of the number. Indeed, such an example highlights the importance of the integrated number to the Bollywood film and suggests that they should be read in terms of the overall perspective of the films rather than as simply something additionally thrown into the mix. Success, and therefore true blockbuster status, depends upon these numbers working within the structure of the film and in a manner that fulfils the audiences knowledge and expectations. The songs are also often used to reflect another key thematic element in the Bachchan blockbuster, that is an overt sympathy with the poor and downtrodden. This element is perhaps most successfully achieved in the Bachchan blockbuster *Muqaddar Ka Sikandar* (1978), but can be seen in a number of other key Bachchan titles such as, for example, *Don* (1978), *Kala Patthar* (1979) and *Hum* (1991).

As the 1980s progressed the tried and tested elements of Bollywood began to change. Amitabh Bachchan was elected to parliament in 1984 representing his home town of Allahabad for the Congress Party, which for a short time shifted the public's focus away from his films. By the late 1980s even his seemingly unassailable star began to wane although he still had some success with films such as such *Hum* (1991) which contained so many familiar elements from his star persona that Rajadhyaksha and Willemen were moved to call it 'a lexicon of Bachchanalia' (1997: 502). Newer stars were beginning to challenge the older stalwarts, and some older stars, such as Bachchan, were beginning to take roles that reflected their ageing and slightly different status within the industry.

The Bachchan influence: *Qurbani* (Feroz Kahn, 1980)

The enormous success of Bachchan's action vehicles meant that other film-makers attempted to make similar types of film and *Qurbani* is a good example of this. Feroz Khan directed, produced and edited the film as well as playing the lead role in this action packed gangster movie. On the surface, there are clear thematic links to the Bachchan films of the late 1970s. Khan plays a motor cycle stuntman turned master safe cracker Rajesh who steals from the rich who, he argues, have only made their money by 'stealing' and exploiting others. Rajesh is a character who shares the distrust of the rich familiar from many of the Bachchan heroes. However, he is also represented as much more of a playboy. Through Khan's performance Rajesh has a knowing edge and a lack of seriousness that one could not imagine Bachchan bringing so explicitly to his lower class heroes, apart from in his more overtly comedic films. Indeed, the humorous edge, familiar from films such as **Amar Akbar Anthony**, is taken further through a strikingly quirky visual style that proves to be very self-conscious with it's jokey jump-cuts and zooms. It is certainly possible to argue that the song and dance numbers, while still relatively few with six, look forward to the visually driven, MTV styles of the 1990s.

The storyline, as one might expect, is familiar: Rajesh falls for night-club singer Shela (Zeenat Aman), but when he is captured by a dogged police officer (played by Amjad Khan) and sent to prison she meets smuggler Amar (Vinod Khanna). The two men later become friends after Rajesh saves Amar's life. The film ends with Amar sacrificing himself for his friend who is left with Shela. The focus on male friendship, the love triangle and the ultimate act of qurbani, show that Thomas is right to argue that familiar storylines, almost clichéd for western viewers, are not problematic for Indian audiences. It is the way the story is delivered through the blockbuster elements: stars, action, songs and dances, exotic locations (the finale is set in Britain) and romance, all wrapped in melodramatic excess, that ensures that the film satisfies its audience and makes it a 'hugely successful action movie' (Rajadhyasha and Willemen 1997: 448). **Qurbani** may be seen as a film that offers some insights into the developments that would occur in the 1980s. Feroz Khan's self-knowing performance, along with that of Amjad Khan, show the levels of self-reflexivity that was entering the mainstream Hindi cinema at the time. While already present in **Amar Akbar Anthony**, within **Qurbani** it is taken to a more consistent level, which looks towards developments in the later 1980s and 1990s.

The performance of Zeenat Aman, as the sultry singer, Shela, also indicates shifts towards more openly sexual heroines.

Again, suggestions of this can be identified in a performance such as Parveen Babi's in *Amar Akbar Anthony*, where she wears more western clothes and reveals more bare flesh than had been the norm earlier in the decade. However, Aman's role is more sustained in the way it does this. She is much more openly 'sexy' and represents a more westernised and 'liberated' version of femininity. Again, this is perhaps best reflected through the musical numbers, here in the most famous song from the film, 'Aap Jaisa Koi', which has her singing in a very western influenced nightclub, wearing short skirts and dancing in slow motion while shaking her hair. More generally *Qurbani*'s music, by the team of Kalyanji and Anandji, is typical of the electronically dominated music of the period. With its popular songs, arresting visuals, popular stars, exotic locations, and stunts *Qurbani* is the perfect example of the blockbuster concept that became a box-office smash.

Monsoon Wedding (Mira Nair, 2001): the Return of Indian Art Cinema?

Monsoon Wedding proved an enormous success in the UK when it was released early in 2002, and this success was repeated across the world. The film marks a re-emergence of a new contemporary Indian art cinema as it had a serious tone and attempted to address a number of issues concerning contemporary Indian society. However, the film also, due to it being set around the preparations for a wedding, shared some

things with the more popular Bollywood films of the 1990s.
Monsoon Wedding was directed by Mira Nair who had already achieved a high international profile with her 1988 *Salaam Bombay!* which drew heavily on her work as a documentary maker. *Salaam Bombay!* links to earlier Indian art films, such as the ground-breaking work of Satyajit Ray, as it tells its story through the character of a young child. Here, Chaipau, a boy, goes to Bombay in search of money to sort out the problems he has left behind at home. The film was awarded the Camera d'Or at the Cannes film festival and an Acadamy Award for Best Foreign Language Film.

Nair followed the success of *Salaam Bombay!* with a $6 million US project *Mississippi Masala* (1991) which starred Denzel Washington. This film was critically well received and Nair stayed in America to make *The Perez Family* (1995) which told the story of Cuban exiles in Miami. This was less successful and Nair returned to India to make *Karma Sutra* (1996) which was partly funded by Channel 4 and co-starred the Bollywood star Rekha. Another lukewarm reception meant that, apart from a US TV movie, *My Own Country* in 1998, Nair produced no major work until *Monsoon Wedding*. The success of this film has led her back to America where she directed a version of *Vanity Fair* (2004) starring Reese Witherspoon and is at the time of writing completing *The Namesake* (2006).

Nair has stated during an interview on the DVD of *Monsoon Wedding* that she wanted to make a film about 'India now. Which is an India that has gone global and dot. com and all kinds of influences are happening now which are very interesting for a traditional community who are in the divide between the old ways and the new.' She does this by setting the story among the intrigues leading up to a large, upper middle class wedding.

The opening of the film sets many of the themes in motion. Following the credits we are introduced to Lalit Verma, the father of the bride who, upon seeing the marigold gate that will be the centre of the wedding celebration is falling apart, becomes concerned that wedding organiser Dubey is not on top of preparations. Inside the house his wife and other women of the family are also preparing. The global element of contemporary middle class India is introduced through the character of Lalit's son who has missed picking up relatives from the US at the airport and claims it is because he is tired as he only returned from Australia the day before. The tradition of the wedding is set against the symbolic contemporality of the family's convergence from all over the Indian diaspora. The conflict between global and traditional cultures is further emphasised in the next scene which introduces the bride Aditi. She is seen working at a television station where a debate about these precise issues is being recorded. Contributors are heard to state that 'just because India has gone global should we embrace everything, what about our ancient culture?' and that 'this is not America, this is India'. We are invited through this sequence to see these issues, that will be addressed through the family wedding, as impacting not just on this family but on many all over the country. This device helps Nair make a film whose themes should be seen as touching not just those characters in the film but which are more universal. The specific manifestations of this conflict are then brought sharply into focus when in the next scene we learn that Aditi is having an affair with the show's presenter. The opposition between tradition (personified by the bride at the arranged wedding) and the modern (the independent young working woman who is sexually active) is complete. The sequence at the television studio skilfully develops the themes that concern the film through the introduction of the characters. In this way the audience is invited to have a greater understanding of them by witnessing how they impact upon these characters while never letting us forget that they are representative of wider society.

Drawing on her background in documentaries Nair approaches the material with an urgency reflected in the film's visual style. The camera often creates the impression of observing, constantly shifting focus. The camerawork and framing therefore heighten a feeling of urgency that suggests both the hustle and bustle of Deli life, but also the chaos of the wedding and more thematically the unfixed and fluid nature of contemporary Indian culture. Here we have a visual style that complements the material on a number of levels again assisting in the creation of depth to the way in which the film handles both its intimate moments and sweeping themes.

The film's ending is also important in that it does offer some conclusions regarding these issues. First, in addressing the hidden history of abuse within the family, Lalit refuses to do what it is suggested is the traditional way to deal with such things – ignore them. He refuses to accept Taj into his home on the day of the wedding even though he knows it may mean his financial ruin. In acting in such a manner he embraces the need to move on and reformulate tradition. The wedding ceremony that follows also marks some other significant concluding moments. Lalit further shows his willingness to change by inviting the lower class wedding organiser Dubey to join in with them as he marries their servant Alice. Dubey himself is representative of a new entreprenural lower class no longer simply willing to accept their lower status. However, not everything at the wedding party is about rejecting the past. During the dance finale with a techno beat playing and all generations together, Rahul is told 'we finally made an Indian out of you,' suggesting that some traditions such as family values should not be lost however far one goes from India.

Much of the success of *Monsoon Wedding* with wider audiences may be down to its ability to meld together contemporary social concerns within the format of the wedding film, which as I have argued was one of the major Bollywood formats in the 1990s. However, the universal theme of the place of family values in a changing world meant that those outside the Indian diaspora could find much to enjoy and engage with in the film.

Bollywood goes global

As already noted over past few years Bollywood has attempted to expand into the global markets represented by the characters in *Monsoon Wedding*. In much of the writing about film there is an assumption that most of the cinema consumed throughout the world emanates from Hollywood. This has led to arguments that assert the cultural dominance of North America, and see film as a form of cultural imperialism. Writers such as Herman and McChesney (1997) use the term globalisation interchangeably with cultural imperialism, with the effect of assuming that this is negative and bringing with it the idea that global media is something that favours the wealthiest nations and their dominant aesthetic codes and conventions. In the case of cinema these are most closely associated with Hollywood.

However, this simplistic model ignores a number of significant national cinemas across the world. As Stuart Hall has argued, 'There are many countervailing tendencies which prevent the world from becoming a culturally uniform and homogenous space' (1997: 211). However, the perceived dominance of Hollywood has worked to mask the cultural flow that already exists. For example, a number of key film practitioners have moved from the Hong Kong industry to work in Hollywood. These have ranged from high profile actors and directors such as Jackie Chan, Jet Li and John Woo, to less 'visible' contributors such as fight choreographers such as Yuen Woo-ping and Corey Yuen, and directors working on less prestige films such as Ronny Yu, Ringo Lam and Tsui Hark. However, it might be argued that their transference has been on Hollywood's terms.

In the case of India there is a stronger sense that the industry has traditionally been satisfied with its domestic and key international markets. Tom O'Reagan has noted that 'along with Hollywood, India is one of the few cinemas that consistently dominate their domestic box-office' (1996: 45). This situation was heightened by the fact that up until the early 1990s there was a ban on dubbing foreign films into Hindi thus preventing any significant encroachment by Hollywood into the domestic market (Hesmondhalgh 2002: 190). For many years popular Hindi cinema had limited markets outside India. These included traditional Diaspora destinations such as Fiji, Mauritius, West and South Africa, as well as countries in the Middle East. Alongside these there were those countries that were looking for cheap, non-Hollywood, products such as those that formed the old eastern bloc. Recently, new markets have begun to appear lucrative for Hindi products. The 'all India' nature of the Hindi language film has meant that emigrants from all over the sub-continent have happily transferred their enthusiasm for Mumbai products to their new homes in the UK, Canada, the US, Australia and New Zealand. The Hindi film industry is therefore faced with a range of new markets that may not all simply want the same product. As Hindi films attempt to appeal to these wider 'geocultural markets', as David Hesmondhalgh (2002: 180) usefully labels them, there have been some significant aesthetic shifts and a marked rise in production values. This would seem logical when these potential 'new' audiences have the choice to consume Hollywood blockbusters as well as films from Mumbai.

The overseas market for Hindi films has been estimated at around $50 million according to 'Screen Daily' and so is a major potential source of profit. This figure is divided predominantly between the US and Canada at 30%, the UK at 25% and the Middle East also at 25%, leaving another 20% from the variety of smaller markets such as those in Australasia. Further evidence of the increasing potential overseas market for popular Hindi films is witnessed by the fact that in October 2002 the Indian Film Exporters association announced they had sold 104 films to the Chinese delegation at the 33rd International Film Festival of India ('Screendaily.com' 7/10/2002). Expansion into these markets will also have an impact on the aesthetic decisions made in production.

While at first these 'geocultural' audiences were happy to receive films from 'home', more recently, there has been clearer distinctions between the films that have proved most popular with audiences in India and those in the western outreaches of the Diaspora such as the UK. For example, 2001's *Khabi Kushi Kabhie Gham*, which as noted above was an enormous hit at the UK box-office, reaching number 3 with a release of 44 prints, while successful in India was outgrossed by the more 'patriotic', and less expensive, *Gadar* (2001). This fact − the difference in tastes in India and the wider markets − has not gone unnoticed and has led some Indian film-makers to begin to tailor their works for this lucrative overseas market. Investors have also noticed the shift. 'Screen International' reported that a group of IT entrepreneurs from India, now based in Silicon valley in the US, have already shown an interest in investing in such products. Furthermore, in January 2003 'Screendaily.com' reported that a group of successful overseas based Indians had hosted a media and entertainment conference in Delhi with a view to raising investment. The higher profile Hindi films, such as *Lagaan*, *Khabi Kushi Kabhie Gham* and *Devdas*, has meant that wealthy business people now see film as a possible area for investment. The trade paper further reported that Amit Khanna, chairman of Reliance Entertainment, has stated that 'India's entertainment industry − film and TV software, animation, post-production, distribution and exhibition businesses - boasts private equity investment worth $200million as of date. Given the interest that the Indian Diaspora has in Bollywood, I see the potential for another $100 million flowing into the industry in the course of the next two years' (Lall 2003: np). With this sort of potential investment Hindi cinema needs to prove it can be taken seriously on a global stage. This is not simple or straightforward for an industry that has developed a reputation for being poorly organised and lacking in a secure industrial infrastructure.

However, for many involved in the industry, the nomination of *Lagaan* in the best foreign film category of the 2002 Academy Awards (Oscars) signalled that Hindi films could now possibly hold their own in a (particular) global context. Although it did not win, the nomination for *Lagaan* did act as a breakout moment for Hindi popular cinema. No longer did those outside the sub-continent see art movies as the only films worthy of consideration produced in India. The prestigious Cannes international film festival proved an equally significant platform for this globalising process. For this reason, producer Bharat Shah and Eros International chose to premiere *Devdas* at Cannes before it opened in Mumbai. This was a significant event which led to Kishore Lulla, chairman of Eros International, to exclaim that 'Bollywood has come of age and we are thrilled to bring this wonderful film to wider audiences internationally.'

Conclusion: *Devdas* at Cannes 2002

© BFI Stills

The premiere of *Devdas* at the 2002 Cannes film festival was a significant moment for the Hindi film industry. After screening films such as *Kabhi Khushi Kabhie Gham* at the marketplace in the past this might be read as a concerted effort to take Hindi cinema overground and into the international arena. Previously, it had only been art or Parallel Cinema films that had arrived at Cannes for official screenings from India. Now *Devdas* was an official selection to be screened out of competition. The change in attitude can be seen by the fact that Sushma Swaraj, Minister of Information and Broadcasting, headed a 100 strong delegation to the festival with the intention of making people take the Hindi popular film industry seriously, one that was concerned and able to deal with export. She stated that in the past Indian film-makers had lacked drive in this area, 'Indian producers were quite satisfied with domestic audiences and profits and with their attitude to the non-resident Indian audience...we now have a new generation of directors who understand that the outside world is watching. This in turn is reflected in what happens on screen' (Frater 2002a: np). Cannes 2002 was an attempt to change this.

The footage of the *Devdas* Cannes premiere on the DVD release makes interesting viewing, particularly when compared to the Mumbai opening. The former saw the films two stars Shah Rhuk Khan and Aishwarya Rai arrive in a horse drawn carriage. The stars and the director Sanjay Bensali then slowly walked up the red carpet stopping for the odd interview and photograph. They then entered the cinema in a manner that can only be described as 'reverent', slowly walking down the aisle and taking their seats as the audience applauded. Everthing designed to signify importance and splendour. In their interviews all three talk of the importance of being at the festival, and their pleasure at *Devdas* being taken seriously by the festival organisers. In contrast the Mumbai opening was much more frenetic and star studded with interviewees being jostled as they speak to the camera and a general assumption that the film is going to be a success. Such assumptions were far removed from the performance at Cannes where the screening was something of a risk.

From Cannes to our local multiplexes to DVD releases, Indian cinema in all its forms is now much more widely available, and has a much higher profile than before. This availability means that we can now use examples of it across our teaching. Below are some suggestions for teaching with and about Indian cinema.

Sample Questions
(Elements of answers in italics.)

Indian cinema offers the opportunity to engage with a number of key concepts within Film and Media Studies. On the one hand, it is a national cinema that can be studied in isolation. On the other, some films may lend themselves to particular syllabus demands, such as *Kuch Kuch Hota Hai* which has been identified in the WJEC A level Film Studies syllabus document. However, as Indian films, particularly those made in Mumbai and labelled Bollywood, gain a higher profile I would suggest that they can, and indeed should, be integrated into course design in a much more wider sense. Therefore I would argue that teachers of film and media can profitably use examples drawn from the cinemas of India to explore a variety of syllabus areas. Below I begin to sketch out how we, as teachers, can develop and expand our teaching by utilising the range of Indian cinema now more widely available, especially on DVD. I have identified key subject areas and suggested a number of titles that might be used in relation to each.

Reading Media/Film Images
Many teachers begin their work with students by introducing approaches to close textual analysis, often under the heading of reading film or media images.

Mise-en-scène
a. **List the elements that make up a film's mise-en-scène.**

b. **Select a short scene from a lavish Bollywood movie, then detail how the director has manipulated the mise-en-scène to make meaning.**

Indian popular cinema can be used to introduce students to the various elements of mise-en-scène. Like Hollywood melodramas, another popular source of examples among teachers, Bollywood is excessive in its use of costume, make-up, lighting and setting, the basic elements of mise-en-scène. A recent example such as **Devdas** *(2002) might be employed by teachers to assist students' understanding of how these elements work together in creating meaning within the frame.* **Devdas** *is particularly useful as it uses mise-en-scène to communicate the differences between characters in terms of social class.*

Semiotics

a. Select 3 images from Indian movies. Identify the
main signs present and discuss their denotation and
connotation.

b. How far are the possible meanings of the signs
culturally specific?

*Students may be introduced to the cultural specificity of film and media
images via Bollywood. Clearly there are certain aspects of meaning within
sequences of a film such as* **Monsoon Wedding** *that are culturally
specific. A simple example, such as the significance of certain flowers and
their relation to 'romance', might be contrasted with the use of Red Roses
in Hollywood films. The difference assisting students to grasp the idea that
images may have 'obvious' meanings that when removed from a specific
context are less than obvious to audiences.*

Genre

a. What are the codes and conventions of Bollywood
movies?

b. Compare and contrast a sequence from a Hollywood
gangster film and a Bollywood gangster film listing the
similarities and differences.

*When we ask students 'what is a genre?' it might be fruitful to give a wider
set of examples than simply those drawn from Hollywood. The specific
interpretations of generic codes and conventions in a context such as India
can shed light on the familiar by placing it into a less familiar setting.
Bollywood offers us more than simply romantic melodramas.*

*I suggest the integration of Indian examples in teaching about, for
example, Gangster films. Alongside films such as* **The Godfather,**
(1971) **Goodfellas** *(1990) and* **Lock, Stock and Two Smoking
Barrels** *(1998) the Bollywood film,* **Company** *(2002) would work very
well. It displays the codes and conventions of the gangster genre, it tracks
the rise and fall of gangland leader, it has shoot-outs, gangsters' molls, etc.,
but takes place in Mumbai and has dance numbers in it. The specific
context becomes important; within Bollywood, one has to expect very
particular additions to the general formula.*

*While there are links with other cinemas such as Hollywood when one
considers gangster films in Indian cinema, there are also genres that are
very particular to India. One such example is the 'mythological' film. Such
works focus on the gods and goddesses, and Gokulsing and Dissanayake
argue:*

One can legitimately say that the mythological film narrating the actions of gods and goddesses is a unique product of the Indian cinema in the way that the Western is of Hollywood. Apart from its own characteristic heroes and villains, gods and demons, immediately recognisable costumes and settings, this genre is informed by a powerful imagination in which good triumphs over evil, so reinforcing the moral order. (1998: 13)

Looking at such genres can throw light on the specifics of our own consumption practices in showing students that some of their most familiar genres might be unfamiliar to other consumers in other parts of the world, and with other cinema experiences.

Popular cinema vs. art cinema

As suggested above, there can be clear differences between the traditions of art cinema and Bollywood. Certain directors, such as Bimal Roy in the 1950s, were seen to introduce art cinema elements into their popular films. The contrast between these traditions can be explored by comparing two films such as **Monsoon Wedding** and **3KG**. Both focus on weddings but offer the chance to discuss the two very different representations of families and weddings, both very much linked to the type of cinema their production is associated with.

Cinema and its relationship with society can be explored through the opposition between art and popular cinema. This may lead to work on the place of cinema in India and the place of Indian cinema in the UK.

Narrative structures

a. **How far do Bollywood films utilise the structures of classical Hollywood narrative cinema?**

b. **List the major differences between the way Bollywood and Hollywood tell stories.**

*Audiences for Bollywood films have a particular expectation in terms of length. Most are nearly three hours long. Students can gain knowledge and understanding of how far western narrative traditions are in themselves conventional by thinking about the differences in structure between Bollywood and Hollywood films. Indian popular cinema often has multiple narrative strands within films, sometimes drawing on traditional epics such as the **Ramayana** and the **Mahabharata**. Students can explore how,* *because of this, audiences are not as driven by enigmas and 'cause and effect' but are more interested in the spectacle of how a familiar story is retold again and again.*

Questions of realism

a. What do you understand by the term 'realism' in relation to cinema?

b. Compare a short sequence from an Indian art film to one from a Bollywood movies. Which one fits the codes and conventions of realism most closely?

Related to work on narrative, Indian cinema can assist in our teaching of non-Hollywood codes and conventions in relation to realism. Again, this can involve work on audiences who do not have the same expectations of believability as those for mainstream fare produced in Hollywood and particularly the UK. Popular cinema generally has operated more broadly than 'serious' cinema, often being criticised for being over-melodramatic or 'unrealistic' in its resolution of plot twists.

Stars

Select a current Bollywood star. How is their persona constructed through a range of media? (Consider their films, promotion and advertising, star portraits, magazine articles etc.)

Most work on stars and stardom focuses on Hollywood. Indian cinema once again offers the opportunity to reflect on the importance of stars in mainstream cinema, but in another production context. In India any film that wants to aim at a mainstream audience needs a star name, often more than one. Stars often work on more than one (sometimes multiple) films at once. Their place, and power, in the industry is vital to its operation. This study can be extended when one considers a star such as Amitabh Bachchan, who for a certain time in the mid-1970s and early 1980s. Bachchan's vehicle **Amar Akbar Anthony** *is a great example of what became known as a multi-star film, as it combined a number of high profile performers in the same film. An excellent recent film that can be used to consider stardom is* **3KG**, *which operates across three generations of Bollywood superstars in casting Bachchan, Shah Rhuk Khan and Hrithtik Roshan.*

Bollywood as a non-western film industry

a. Compare the Mumbai premiere of *Devdas* (available on DVD) to those you have seen for Hollywood films. List the similarities and differences, what do they tell us about the respective industries?

b. List the countries that show Bollywood films. Do you think that that has changed over the past 30 years? Why might this change have occured, and do you think it has had an impact on the Bollywood film industry?

The Bollywood production process offers the chance to consider the way in which non-Hollywood industries are organised. Detailed information on these areas can be obtained from some of the extensive web-sites devoted to Bollywood. A particularly good resource is www.cyberbollywood.com, which offers information on the territories and distribution patterns in India. Students can be encouraged to explore the differences to Hollywood that Bollywood offers. The more make-piece financing again offers useful test cases in production.

*Bollywood's recent expansion into western markets can be linked to questions of global film markets, and in particular the ways in which Indian companies such as Yash Raj might be argued to have begun to angle their products at non-resident Indian (NRI) audiences. Indeed, on a more ambitious note, Bollywood is a way into thinking about cinematic global exchange, particularly in terms of its remakes of Hollywood successes and the appearance of the Amir Khan who starred in **Lagaan** at the Oscars and the gala opening of **Devdas** at Cannes.*

Teaching Resources

There are a number of film magazines devoted to Indian popular cinema. The most widely available is 'Stardust', which, as the title suggests, focuses on Indian film stars. Another useful publication is 'CineBlitz'. Asian press titles such as 'Eastern Eye' carry regular reviews and interviews with Bollywood stars.

There are a wide range of web-sites devoted to 'Bollywood', such as www.cyberbollywood.com, that have information about the latest releases in India, box-office figures, etc. South Asian cable and satellite channels, available in the UK, carry Bollywood programmes that preview films and discuss stars lives.

Films are increasingly available on the high street in subtitled versions, mainly on DVD. Recent successes such as **Devdas**, **3KG** and **Lagaan** are widely available at certain HMV and Virgin stores, as are older favourites such as **Dilwale Dulhania Le Jayenge** and **Kuch Kuch Hota Hai**. Art house titles such as Ray's **Apu** trilogy have recently appeared on DVD from the British Film Institute. It is hoped that with Indian cinemas increased profile that more and more titles will appear. Many are available from specialist outlets on the internet. Specialists such as Eros Entertainment (www.erosentertainment.com) and Moviemail (wwwmoviem.co.uk) carry extensive lists, but others such as play.com also have substantial holdings.

Select Filmography

Art cinema

Film	Stars	Teaching interest	Availablilty
Apu Trilogy (Satyajit Ray) **Pather Panchali** (1955) **Aparajito** (1956) **The World of Apu** (1959)		Ray's landmark works that establishes Indian art cinema internationally	Artificial Eye DVD. English subtitles
A River Called Titas (Ritwik Ghatak 1973)	Rosy Somad	Classic humanist film	BFI DVD. English subtitles
The Name of the River (Anup Singh 1992)		Bio-pic of Art Film maker Ritwik Ghatak	BFI DVD. English subtitles
The Terrorist (Santosh Sivan 1999)	Ayesha Dharkar	Political film in which a young woman volunteers to become a suicide bomber	Tartan DVD. English subtitles

Bollywood

Film	Stars	Teaching interest	Availablilty
Devdas (Bimal Roy 1955)	Starring Dilip Kumar and Vyjayantimala	Earlier version of recent hit. Mixes song and dance conventions with touches of realism.	Yash Raj Films DVD. English subtitles.
Mother India (Mehboob 1957)	Starring Nargis, Sunil Dutt, Rajendra Kumar and Raaj Kumar.	Early super hit. Highly influencial and epic in scope.	DEI (Digital Entertainment Inc.) DVD. English subtitles.
Deewaar (Yash Chopra 1975)	Starring Amitabh Bachchan and Shashi Kapoor	All time classic urban melodrama. Hugely influential on 1970s Bollywood.	Eros International DVD. English subtitles.
Sholay (Ramesh Sippy 1975)	Starring Amitabh Bachchan	Often described as a 'curry' western. Again highly influential action movie. One of the all time most popular Bollywood movies.	Eros International DVD. English subtitles
Qurbani (Feroz Khan 1980)	Starring Feroz Khan, Vinod Khanna and Amjad Khan	Bachchan influenced action with two guys falling for Zeenat Aman.	Eros International DVD. English subtitles.
Hum Aapke Hain Koun! (Sooraj R. Barjatya 1994)	Starring Madhuri Dixit and Salman Khan	Massive hit that spawned many wedding set stories.	Eros International DVD. English subtitles.
Bombay (Mani Ratnam 1995)	Starring Arvind Swamy and Manisha Koirala	Film that mixes serious content – it is set during 1992 riots – and memorable songs.	Eros International DVD. English subtitles.
Dilwale Dulhania Le Jayenge (Aditya Chopra 1995)	Starring Shah Rukh Khan, Kajol and Amrish Puri	Romantic mega hit partly set in London.	Yash Raj Films DVD. English subtitles.
Kuch Kuch Hota Hai (Karan Johar 1998)	Starring Shah Rukh Khan, Kajol and Rani Mukerji	Another enormous hit with youthful flavour.	Yash Raj Films DVD. English subtitles.
Devdas (Sanjay Leela Bhansali 2001)	Starring Shah Rukh Khan, Madhuri Dixit and Aishwarya Rai	Blockbuster version of famous story. Star vehicle with lavish production values.	Eros International DVD. English subtitles.

Select Bibliography

Art cinema

Armes, R. *Third World Film Making and the West*. Berkeley: University of California Press, 1987.

Chakravarty, Sumita S. (ed.) *The Enemy Within: The films of Mrinal Sen*. Trowbridge: Flicks Books, 2000.

Datta, S. *Shyam Benegal*. London: BFI, 2002.

Hood, J. W. *The Essential Mystery: Major Filmmakers of Indian Art Cinema*. London: Sangam Books, 2000.

Williams, F. 'The Art Film in India: A Report on Mrinal Sen' in Sumita S. Chakravarty (ed.) *The Enemy Within: The Films of Mrinal Sen*. Trowbridge: Flicks Books, 2000.

Bollywood / popular cinema

Banker, A. *Bollywood*. Herts: Pocket Essentials, 2001.

Chakaravarty, Sumita S. *National Identity in Indian Popular Cinema, 1947 -1987*. Austin: University of Texas Press, 1993.

Chatterjee, G. *Mother India*. London: BFI, 2002.

Chopra, A. *Dilwale Dulhania Le Jayenge*. London: BFI, 2002.

Deme, S. *Movies, Masculinity and Modernity: An Ethnography of Men's Filmgoing in India*. Westport: Greenwood Press, 2000.

Dissanayake, W. 'The Concept of Evil and Social Order in Indian Melodrama: An Evolving Dialectic' in W. Dissanayake (ed.) *Melodrama and Asian Cinema*. Cambridge: Cambridge University Press, 1993.

Dwyer, R. *Yash Chopra*. London: BFI, 2002.

Dwyer, R. and Patel, D. Cinema *India: The Visual Culture of Hindi Film*. London: Reaktion Books, 2002.

Frater, P. 'Focus Picks Up *Devdas* Sales Duties' Screendaily.com 18 May 2002.

Gandy, B. and Thomas, R. 'Three Indian Film Stars' in C. Gledhill (ed.) Stardom: *Industry of Desire*. London: Routledge, 1991.

Gokulsing, K.M. and Dissanayake, W. *Indian Popular Cinema: A narrative of Cultural Change*. Stoke-on-Trent: Trentham Books, 1998.

Gopalan, L. *Cinema of Interruptions: Action Genre in Contemporary Indian Cinema*. London: BFI, 2002.

Kabir, N.M. *Bollywood: The Indian Cinema Story*. London: Channel 4 Books, 2001.

Lall, B. 'Expat Indians Plan to Raise Funds for Bollywood Productions' *Screendaily.com* 14 January 2003.

Mishra, V. 'Towards a Theoretical Critique of Bombay Cinema' *Screen* 26 (3-4), 1985: 133-46.

Mishra, V. *Bollywood Cinema: Temples of Desire*. London: Routledge, 2002.

Sharma, A. 'Blood, Sweat and Tears: Amitabh Bachchan, Urban Demi-god' in P. Kirkham and J. Thumin (eds) *You Tarzan: Masculinity, Movies and Men*. London: Lawrence and Wishart, 1993.

Thomas, R. 'Indian Cinema: Pleasures and Popularity' *Screen* 26 (3-4), 1985: 116 -32.

Vasudevan, R.S. 'The Melodramatic Mode and the Commercial Hindi Cinema: Notes on Film History, Narrative and Performance in the 1950s' *Screen 30* (3), 1989: 29-50.

Vasudevan, R.S. (ed.) *Making Meaning in Indian Cinema*. New Deli: Oxford University Press, 2000.

Vasudevan, Ravi S. 'The Politics of Cultural Address in a 'Transitional' Cinema' in C. Gledhill and L. Williams (eds) *Reinventing Film Studies*. London: Arnold, 2000.

General

Bordwell, D. 'The Art Cinema as a Mode of Film Practice' *Film Criticism* 4 (1), 1979.

Hall, S. 'The Centrality of Culture: Notes on the Cultural Revolutions of our Time' in K. Thompson (ed.) *Media and Cultural Regulation*. London: Sage, 1997.

Herman, E.S. and McChesney, R.W. *The Global Media*. London: Cassell.

Hesmondhalgh, D. *The Cultural Industries*. London: Sage.

O'Reagan, T. *Australian National Cinema*. London: Routledge.

Rajadhyaksha, A. and Willemen, P. *Encyclopaedia of Indian Cinema: New Revised Edition*. London: British Film Institute, 1999.

Rao, L. 'Woman in Indian Films: A Paradigm of Continuity and Change' *Media, Culture and Society* 11, 1989: 443, 458.

Thompson, K. and Bordwell, D. *Film History: An Introduction* (2nd edition). New York: Mcgraw Hill, 2003.

Wyatt, Justin. *High Concept: Movies and Marketing in Hollywood* Austin: University of Texas Press, 1994